IMAGES
*of America*

# THE HISTORIC CORE
## OF LOS ANGELES

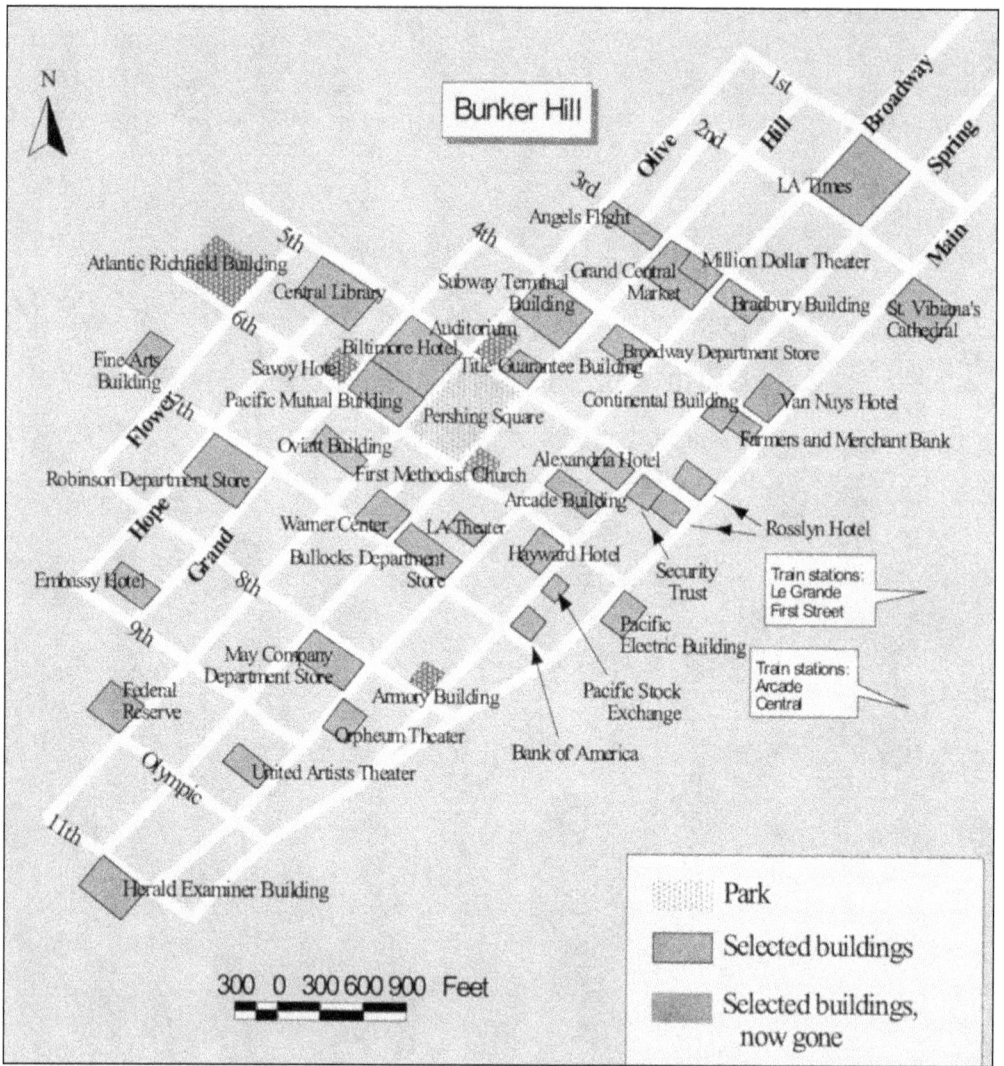

## Map Labels

**N**

Bunker Hill

1st
Olive   2nd
Hill   Broadway
Spring
LA Times
3rd
Angels Flight
Main
5th
4th
Atlantic Richfield Building
Grand Central   Million Dollar Theater
Central Library
Subway Terminal   Market
Building
Bradbury Building   St. Vibiana's
6th
Auditorium   Cathedral
Biltimore Hotel
Fine Arts   Savoy Hotel   Title Guarantee Building   Broadway Department Store
Building
Pacific Mutual Building   Continental Building   Van Nuys Hotel
Flower   7th
Pershing Square   Farmers and Merchant Bank
Oviatt Building
Robinson Department Store   First Methodist Church   Alexandria Hotel
Arcade Building
Hope
Warner Center   LA Theater   Rosslyn Hotel
Bullocks Department   Hayward Hotel
Embassy Hotel   Grand   8th   Store   Security   Train stations:
Trust   Le Grande
9th   First Street
May Company   Pacific
Department Store   Electric Building
Federal   Armory Building   Train stations:
Reserve   Pacific Stock   Arcade
Olympic   Orpheum Theater   Exchange   Central
United Artists Theater   Bank of America
11th

Herald Examiner Building

300   0   300 600 900   Feet

Park

Selected buildings

Selected buildings,
now gone

This 2004 map of the Historic Core shows the location of some of the landmarks discussed in the book. Many of the Core's stately buildings are currently undergoing renovation for new cultural, commercial, and residential use. (Courtesy of G. DeVerteuil.)

IMAGES
*of America*

# THE HISTORIC CORE
## OF LOS ANGELES

Curtis C. Roseman, Ruth Wallach,
Dace Taube, Linda McCann,
and Geoffrey DeVerteuil

ARCADIA
PUBLISHING

Published by Arcadia Publishing
Charleston, South Carolina


Library of Congress Catalog Card Number: 2004110478

For all general information contact Arcadia Publishing at:
Telephone 843-853-2070
Fax 843-853-0044
E-mail sales@arcadiapublishing.com
For customer service and orders:
Toll-Free 1-888-313-2665

Visit us on the Internet at www.arcadiapublishing.com

Biddy Mason was born a slave in 1818, won her freedom in court in 1856, and became a successful Los Angeles nurse, midwife, and entrepreneur. With her earnings she was able to acquire land on Spring Street in downtown Los Angeles. A charter member of the First African Methodist Episcopal Church of Los Angeles, she died in 1891. (Courtesy of L. McCann.)

# CONTENTS

# ABOUT THE AUTHORS

Curtis C. Roseman is a professor of geography at the University of Southern California. His research interests include the migration and settlement of ethnic populations and American cities' downtowns. With Geoffrey DeVerteuil, he has developed a web site on downtown Los Angeles: www.usc.edu/dept/geography/losangeles/lawalk/. Roseman wrote the introduction and the Main Street and Spring Street chapters.

Ruth Wallach is the head of the Architecture and Fine Arts Library at the University of Southern California. She maintains a web site on public art in Los Angeles (www.usc.edu/isd/archives/la/pubart). Wallach wrote the chapter on Hill Street.

Dace Taube is the Regional History Collection librarian for Specialized Libraries and Archival Collections at the University of Southern California. She manages various manuscript collections and three notable photographic collections, which document 100 year of Southern California history. Taube wrote the Broadway Street chapter.

Linda McCann is a member of the library faculty at the University of Southern California and is the project director of the Los Angeles Comprehensive Bibliographic Database. She co-authors the web site, "Los Angeles: Past, Present & Future" (www.usc.edu/isd/archives/la/). McCann wrote the Pershing Square, Olive Street, and West chapter.

Geoffrey DeVerteuil is assistant professor of geography at the University of Manitoba. His research specialty is urban geography; he lived in Los Angeles from 1995 through 2001. DeVerteuil is responsible for the maps.

# ACKNOWLEDGMENTS

This book would not have been possible without the generous support of the Information Services Division at the University of Southern California, which allowed use of its collections and provided digital reproductions. The authors wish to thank the following for their enthusiastic support and help: John Ahouse, Matt Gainer, Elizabeth Roseman, Robert C. Michelson, Andrew H. Nelson, John Taube Sr., and Claude Zachary.

# INTRODUCTION

This book tells the story of the evolution of the early 20th-century "Historic Core" of downtown Los Angeles. Los Angeles grew from a small village of 11,000 people in 1880 to a city of over 100,000 in 1900; thereafter it grew rapidly to become a major metropolis of the 20th century. In the late 19th century, the emerging city built a dense core of downtown business and government buildings south of the plaza and north of about Second Street, the location of today's civic center. After the turn of the century, growth of the downtown extended rapidly to the south and west into what is now called the Historic Core. By 1930, a classic American central business district had developed here. By the middle of the 20th century, civic center government buildings and plazas had replaced most of the older 19th-century core. Our purpose is to describe, through images and their captions, the roots and evolution of the Historic Core of the 20th-century downtown area, its major functions and activities, and its structures and environments.

In traditional 20th-century downtowns, even in sprawling Los Angeles, people did "everything." They patronized big department stores, specialty shops, movie houses, restaurants, and hotels. A complete range of services (doctors, dentists, lawyers, real estate and insurance agents, etc.) was located in the upper floors of these buildings. Until the 1950s, downtown Los Angeles was connected to the rest of the urban area by two extensive trolley systems, the Yellow Cars that plied the streets of the City of Los Angeles, and the Red Cars that ran to neighboring towns on what was the largest inter-urban rail system in the United States. Beginning in the 1920s, automobiles contributed to the decline of these systems while suburban sprawl led to the gradual decline of downtown Los Angeles.

Almost every building in the Historic Core was built between 1900 and 1930. With few exceptions they still stand today. Still in evidence are old department stores, theaters, hotels, institutions, and office buildings. They were built in a variety of architectural styles and include many significant art deco designs. Most of these historic buildings are exactly 150 feet in height, the result of a city limit on height imposed in 1904, giving the area a special visual feel. The lack of tall buildings, up until the 1960s, also contributed to an incorrect assumption, held by Angelinos as well as outsiders, that Los Angeles did not have a downtown. It did!

We have organized the book geographically from east to west, keying on five main north-south streets that traverse the 20th-century Historic Core: Main, Spring, Broadway, Hill, and Olive. Each of these streets anchors a chapter. Each chapter describes the evolution of downtown environments along its street in the Historic Core. To varying degrees each chapter also develops topical themes that are in some way anchored or inspired by its street. Collectively these themes highlight the major activities of this traditional American downtown area.

The first chapter, "Main Street and East: Arriving and Staying in Downtown," features a travel theme. The early railroad and trolley terminals that brought people into downtown were located on or east of this street, along with a number of major hotels in which visitors stayed. After rail traffic was consolidated some distance away at Union Station in 1938, the hostelry of the Main Street area gradually declined in importance. Many of the smaller hotels disappeared, although several of the larger ones remain today.

The next chapter, "Spring Street: The Wall Street of the West" focuses on the banking institutions that lined the street for most of the 20th century. A number of these old bank buildings are now part of the Spring Street Historic District, recognized on the National Register of Historic Places. This chapter also explores the evolution of tall buildings in downtown Los Angeles, the first in the Historic Core being the 1903 Continental Building at Fourth and Main.

"Broadway: The Great White Way" highlights two broad sets of activities, entertainment and shopping, that made this the most famous street in downtown Los Angeles. Major vaudeville and movie houses are described, 12 of which survive and are listed on the National Historic Register, as are major downtown department stores; several of the largest having been on Broadway. In addition, the chapter briefly traces the evolution and movement of major newspapers.

"Hill Street: The City Spills Over" emphasizes the transition from residential to commercial activities in downtown Los Angeles. One by one, both large and small residences were replaced by businesses along the street, including hotels, stores, and buildings that comprise the present-day Jewelry District. Hill Street was connected to the residential areas of Bunker Hill by two funicular rails, Angels Flight (in operation again since 1996) and Court Flight.

A central theme of the final chapter, "Pershing Square, Olive Street, and West," is the evolution of Pershing Square (called Central Park from 1866 to 1918), which is the largest downtown Los Angeles park and was a primary locus for downtown public gatherings through the first two-thirds of the 20th century. Also featured are a variety of institutions, including the central library, schools, clubs, and churches, which were (and to some extent still are) clustered around Pershing Square.

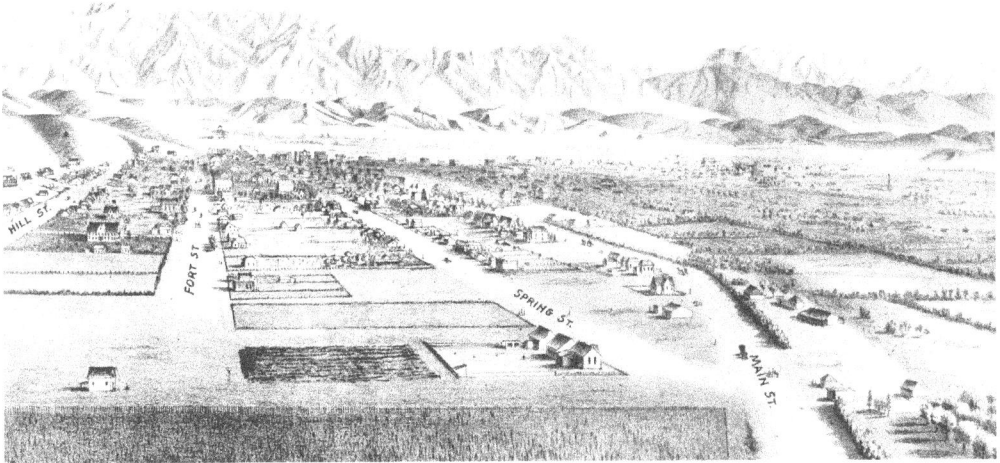

This 1873 lithograph shows the basic pattern of streets in what would become the Historic Core (Fort Street later became Broadway). Los Angeles was a small village of about 6,000 people, compared to over 150,000 living in San Francisco. This view looks northeast to the San Gabriel Mountains from today's Olympic Boulevard (Ninth Street). (Courtesy of CHS.)

This early 1920s photograph shows that the area had grown into a major downtown. Many of the important buildings in the Historic Core had already been built, although others would be completed in the late 1920s and early 1930s. In the lower center is the Los Angeles *Examiner* Building at Eleventh and Broadway. (Courtesy of CHS.)

Calle de Etermidad (Street of Eternity), the 1993 mural by Johanna Poethig, includes a variety of images related to the Latino community in the area. The arms that reach to the sky are based on ancient Peruvian metal work, and the Aztec calendar contains text by the poet Octavio Paz on time, place, home, and exile. The mural, shown here in a 1998 photograph, is located at 351 South Broadway. (Courtesy of R. Wallach.)

# One

# MAIN STREET AND EAST
## ARRIVING AND STAYING IN DOWNTOWN

For five decades following the 1880s, the railroad depots located east of Main Street provided the primary connection between Los Angeles and the rest of the United States. By 1900 several smaller lines had been consolidated under three large railroad companies, the Southern Pacific, Santa Fe, and the Union Pacific, each of which had established a depot a few blocks east of Main Street. As the core of the central business district migrated southward from what is now the civic center area, many of the modern, 20th-century hotels were established on Main and adjacent streets to be accessible to those depots. Some of them are still standing, including the Rosslyn, Frontier, Van Nuys, Alexandria, Hayward, and El Rey. In 1939, all intercity rail traffic was consolidated at Union Station, located a few blocks north of the depots that it replaced.

During the first half of the 20th century, another rail system, the Red Cars of the Pacific Electric interurban rail system, connected downtown Los Angeles to the urban region, including the San Fernando Valley, Long Beach, and San Bernardino. Two of the Red Car terminals, the Pacific Electric Building on Main and the Subway Terminal Building on Hill Streets, became major focal points of activity in downtown and remain today as significant historical landmarks.

After World War II, both intercity and interurban rail rapidly declined in importance relative to automobile travel. Because of this, and because of competition from new hotels west of the Historic Core, the hotels on and near Main Street became less attractive to many business and pleasure travelers. After World War II, Main Street continued to reflect its history as a hotel district, with a street life that included bars, adult theaters, and bookstores. In the latter half of the 20th century the area east of Main Street was the core of skid row, and some of the hotels became single-room occupancy facilities that served the poor and the periodic homeless. At the beginning of the 21st century, Main Street began to experience a turnaround, as several of its large historic buildings were converted to residential lofts, bringing many new residents to the area.

The station pictured above c. 1880 was the downtown terminus for the first railroad in the region, the Los Angeles and San Pedro, which later became part of the Southern Pacific Railroad. Completed in September 1869, the San Pedro line extended straight south from downtown Los Angeles to the location of today's port. The station, which was destroyed by fire in 1924, was located just south of today's Union Station. (Courtesy of CHS.)

Another early railroad was the Los Angeles and Independence, which ran from downtown to Santa Monica. Its station, pictured at left, was located on San Pedro Street between Fourth and Fifth Streets, several blocks closer to Main Street than the depots built later. It was destroyed by fire in November 1888. (Courtesy of CHS.)

Sometimes known as the First Street Depot, the Salt Lake and Union Pacific Depot originally served the Los Angeles Terminal Railroad System, which ran south to Terminal Island at what is now the Port of Los Angeles. Originally built in 1891, the depot later served the Los Angeles and Salt Lake Railroad, which eventually became part of the Union Pacific Railroad. In 1917 the Union Pacific attempted, without success, to abandon this station and share with the Southern Pacific its relatively new (1914) Central Station. In poor shape by the time of this early 1920s photograph, First Street Depot was destroyed by fire in late 1924, after which the Union Pacific did move to Central Station. The two railroads continued to share Central Station until both moved to the new Union Station in 1939. (Courtesy of CHS.)

In 1893 the Atchison, Topeka, and Santa Fe Railroad opened the Moorish-style La Grande Station along the Los Angeles River on Santa Fe Avenue between First and Second Streets. Like many Santa Fe stations across the West, this one included a Harvey House restaurant, opened here in 1900. This famous chain of restaurants employed uniformed "Harvey Girls" as waitresses, famous also for the 1946 Judy Garland MGM movie, *The Harvey Girls*, which featured the Oscar-winning song, "Do ya hear that whistle down the line? / I figure that it's engine No. 49. / She's the only one that'll sound that way. / On the Atchison, Topeka and the Santa Fe." (Courtesy of CHS.)

This 1909 panoramic view shows the location of the Santa Fe's La Grande Station and the Union Pacific's First Street Depot (identified here as the "Salt Lake Route"). The First Street Viaduct spanning the Los Angeles River carried both trolley lines and private vehicles. The area west of the Santa Fe station is dominated by commercial buildings containing mostly wholesale businesses, a number of which are still there today. Quite a few residences can be seen on both sides of the river. Not many hotels are nearby, the Wheeler being the closest. The area around these depots contrasts to the neighborhood of the Southern Pacific Arcade Depot a few blocks away, where many small hotels are located. In the middle foreground of this map is the northern part of the Santa Fe Freight Depot, built in 1907. Today it is home of the Southern California Institute of Architecture. (Courtesy of the Library of Congress.)

In 1881 the Southern Pacific Railroad was the first to complete a transcontinental line directly to Los Angeles. Replacing earlier and smaller stations, the Southern Pacific built the Arcade Station in 1888, shown in this c. 1895 photo. Located between Alameda Boulevard and Central Avenue, between Fourth and Fifth Streets, it was used by the Southern Pacific until 1914. (Courtesy of CHS.)

This 1889 photo shows a San Pedro palm being brought to the Arcade Depot. The palm is prominently displayed in most extant images of the Santa Fe Railroad Depot. (Courtesy of CHS.)

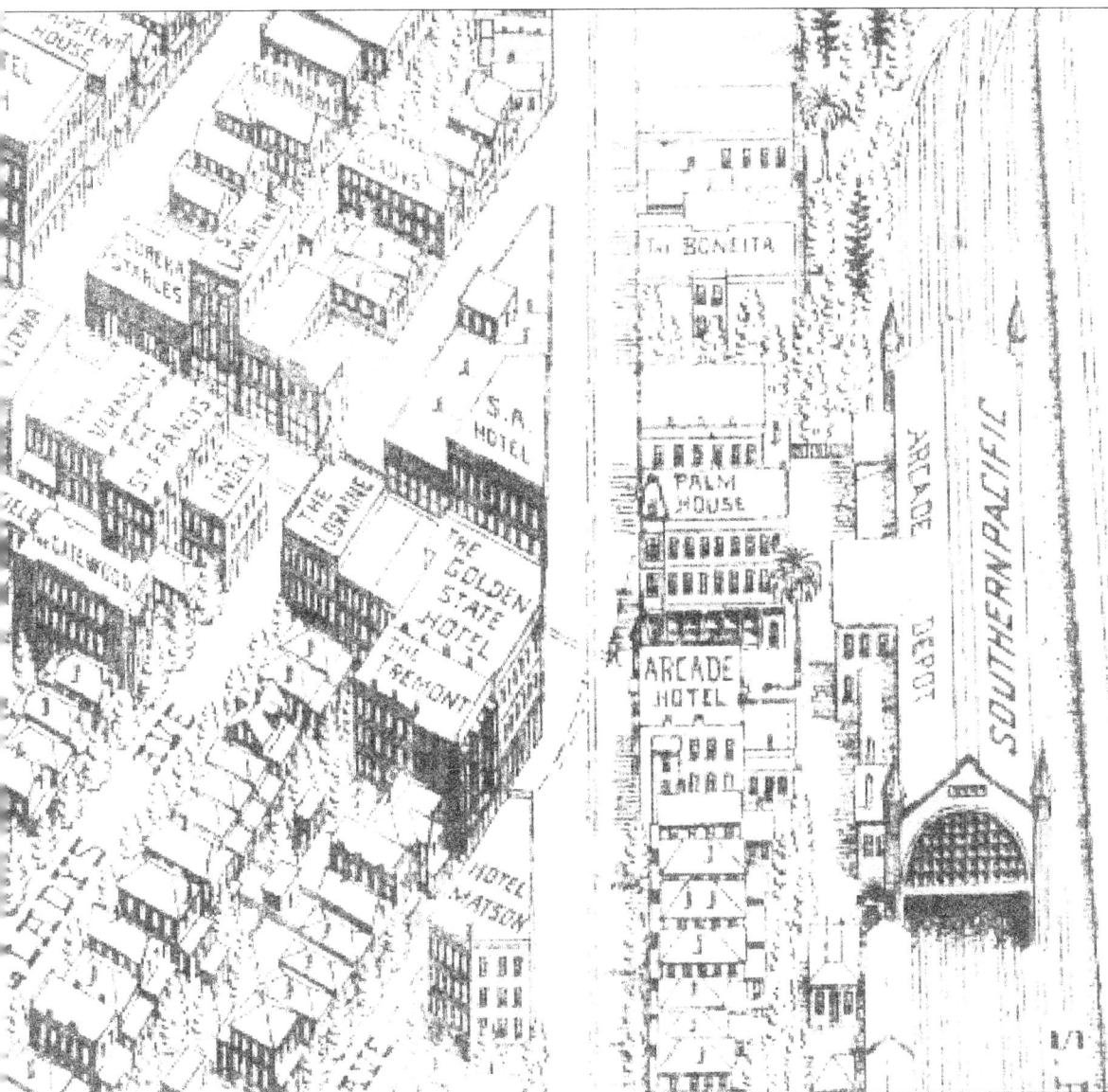

This 1909 panoramic map shows the location of the Arcade Depot. The tracks ran through its large shed along Alameda Boulevard. In fact, the Southern Pacific tracks ran down the middle of Alameda through the entire length of downtown Los Angeles, competing for space with carriages, trolleys, and automobiles. In contrast to the site of the Santa Fe and Union Pacific depots, both located on the Los Angeles River, this site had many hotels, quite a few of which are identified on this panorama. Note how the Arcade and the Palm House Hotels flanked the depot's main entrance leading to Fifth Street. These two hotels, along with virtually all structures on the west side of the depot, would later be razed to make room for the 1914 Southern Pacific Central Depot. (Courtesy of the Library of Congress.)

The Southern Pacific Railroad built Central Station in 1914 to replace the 26-year-old Arcade Depot. It was built essentially in front (to the west) of the Arcade station so that the new station fronted directly on Central Avenue. As a result, several residences and hotels were razed to make room for the new station. Central Station and its predecessor, Arcade Depot, were several blocks closer to the Historic Core than the Santa Fe and Union Pacific depots. In the foreground of this 1924 photo are trolleys, automobiles, and jitneys (predecessors to taxis) that connected the station to the Historic Core a few blocks to the west. The Los Angeles Ice and Cold Storage Company can be seen in the background. (Courtesy of CHS.)

The Union Pacific Railroad shared Central Station with the Southern Pacific beginning in 1924, after its First Street Depot burned down. Both railroads then moved to the new Union Station in 1939. This 1930s photo of Central Station shows signs for both Union Pacific and Southern Pacific Railroads above the tall, arched windows. (Courtesy of the *Examiner*.)

Central Station's interior, shown in this 1930s photo, is reminiscent of many of the other grand American railroad stations of the time. It was, however, quite a bit smaller than most big city stations, and intercity passenger service eventually moved to the much larger Union Station. (Courtesy of the *Examiner*.)

Union Station was completed in 1939 as the last great rail terminal in the United States, consolidating passenger trains of the Southern Pacific, Santa Fe, and Union Pacific Railroads. The older stations located a mile or so south of Union Station were turned to other uses and eventually razed. The Terminal Annex Post Office is shown in the background of this photo. (Courtesy of CHS.)

This 1931 photo shows the site of Union Station, which included the Chinatown of the time and its hundreds of homes, institutions, and stores. Lacking political power, the Chinese were forced to move a few blocks northwest to a "new" Chinatown to accommodate the building of this new rail terminal. Today's Chinatown dates back to that move in the 1930s. (Courtesy of CHS.)

Union Station was opened on May 3, 1939 to a celebration that attracted hundreds of thousands of people. Pictured here is part of the crowd and a vintage passenger car pulled by Southern Pacific's 1869 No. 1 locomotive. The train is on Alameda Avenue in front of Union Station, which had been used for decades for intercity trains. (Courtesy of CHS.)

This 945 photo shows servicemen gathered at Union Station. Because Los Angeles played such a pivotal role in World War II, particularly after the Japanese attack at Pearl Harbor, Union Station was a very busy place during the war. However, after the 1940s, with the rapidly expanding use of the automobile, intercity passenger rail traffic declined precipitously across the United States as well as at Union Station. Today it is an important hub of commuter rail, light rail, and subway lines. (Courtesy of AAA.)

The Pacific Electric Building on Sixth and Main Streets, completed in 1908, was the tallest business building west of the Mississippi River and the focal point for the interurban trolleys, the Red Cars. Hundreds of cars departed daily for destinations throughout Los Angeles, Riverside, and San Bernardino counties. Also sometimes known as the Huntington Building, it served as the main headquarters for the Pacific Electric Railway Company, headed by Henry Huntington. Whereas some of the Red Cars entered the front of the building, most of them entered a lower level at the rear of the building where the Pacific Electric Sixth Street Station was previously located. In the basement of the Pacific Electric Building along Sixth Street is Cole's Pacific Electric Buffet, which claims to be the oldest continuously operating restaurant and saloon in Los Angeles, having opened in 1908. Inside Cole's are numerous historical photos of the building and of Red Cars, along with route maps and other memorabilia of the Pacific Electric interurban system. The Pacific Electric Building was converted to residential lofts in the early 2000s, along with a number of other buildings in the neighborhood. (Courtesy of CHS.)

About the same time the Pacific Electric Railway Company built its terminal on Sixth and Main Streets in 1908 to serve interurban lines from the east and south, it established this Hill Street Station at Fourth Street to serve the lines from the north and west. This station was replaced by the Subway Terminal Building in late 1925. Part of the new Biltmore Hotel can be seen in the upper left-hand corner of this 1925 photo. (Courtesy of CHS.)

Opened in November 1925 by the Pacific Electric Railway Company, the Subway Terminal Building served as both an office building and a Pacific Electric Red Car terminal. Just prior to its opening, a new mile-long tunnel was bored under Bunker Hill for service to Hollywood and San Fernando Valley, Glendale, and Burbank. Red Car service out of this station ended in the year of this photo, 1955. (Courtesy of Whittington.)

The Saint Elmo Hotel, shown in this c. 1890 photo, was located at the site of today's Los Angeles City Hall. Now the site of the civic center, this area was a dense core of commercial and government buildings in the late 19th century. Through the first half of the 20th century most of the buildings in this area, including the Saint Elmo, were replaced by city, county, state, and federal government buildings and plazas. (Courtesy of CHS.)

This c. 1888 photo shows St. Vibiana's Cathedral at Second and Main. Completed in 1880, St. Vibiana's predated most of the larger 19th-century commercial and government buildings. It remained the central edifice of the Los Angeles Catholic Archdiocese until 1995 when it was closed owing to damage from the 1994 Northridge earthquake. It was replaced by the new Cathedral of Our Lady of the Angeles at Temple and Grand, which was dedicated in 2002. (Courtesy of CHS.)

One of many hotels in the area, the Hotel Gray, shown in this c. 1905 photo, was on the southern edge of the dense, late-19th-century downtown, on the northeast corner of Third and Main Streets. Note the awnings used by the west-facing ground floor store windows, and the striped cloth awnings on the upper floor windows, especially on those facing south. A variety of businesses were located on the ground floor. (Courtesy of CHS.)

Opposite the Gray, at the southeast corner of Third and Main Streets, was the Hotel Florence, shown in this photograph taken between 1900 and 1905. Cameron E. Thom, who was mayor of Los Angeles from 1882 to 1884, lived in a house behind the hotel on Third Street. (Courtesy of CHS.)

The Westminster Hotel was located at the northeast corner of Fourth and Main Streets, a large Victorian brick building with a six-story tower. In this c. 1900 photo, a variety of street-level retail stores can be seen, as well as awnings protecting south-facing windows. This is the only historic building to have been razed at the corner of Fourth and Main. Remaining today on the other three corners are the Barclay (Van Nuys) Hotel, the Farmers and Merchants Bank, and the San Fernando Building. (Courtesy of CHS.)

The Van Nuys Hotel was brand new in this 1885 photo. Located across Main Street from the Westminster, the Van Nuys was one of the first of a new generation of modern hotels built south of the old center of Los Angeles. Developed by Isaac Newton Van Nuys, who founded the community of Van Nuys, it boasted electricity and telephones in every room. (Courtesy of CHS.)

This c. 1924 photo shows a busy corner of Fourth and Main Streets, looking north. In the foreground on the left and right, respectively, are the Farmers and Merchants Bank and the San Fernando Building, both of which were renovated in the early 2000s as part of the Old Bank District, a residential loft development. The other two buildings are the Van Nuys (Barclay) and Westminster Hotels. Of these four buildings, only the Westminster is gone today. In the distance on the left side of Main Street is the Higgins Building, which was built in 1911 and restored in the early 2000s. (Courtesy of CHS.)

This c. 1917 photograph looks south on Main from the Westminster Hotel tower at Fourth Street. In the left foreground is the San Fernando Building. Across Main Street are the Farmers and Merchants Bank and the Isaias Hellman Building, all of which are part of the Old Bank District residential development. Beyond the Hellman is Barker Brothers furniture store, and in the distance are three buildings that comprised the Rosslyn Hotel. Notable in the photo is one of the Rosslyn's large building-top signs facing east toward the railroad stations. Visible at street level are awnings that shaded first floor businesses from the morning sun. By 1917 the trolleys on Main and other downtown areas shared the streets with automobiles. (Courtesy of CHS.)

By the mid-1920s the Rosslyn Hotel had expanded to include two large buildings, a 1913 one on the north side of Fifth Street (on the right) and a 1923 annex on the south side. The firm of John Parkinson designed both. The two buildings complement one another both in their matching Beaux-Arts styles and through the massive signs atop their roofs. In the 1920s and 1930s the hotel boasted that it was the largest on the Pacific Coast, with 1,100 rooms and a marble subway connecting the two buildings. One postcard proclaimed the Rosslyn to be located "in the heart of Los Angeles, Fifth and Main." This 2004 photo shows the Rosslyn with two of the financial district's skyscrapers in the background about five blocks to the west, both completed in the early 1990s. The shorter is the Gas Company Tower, the top of which is said to suggest a ship approaching the "lighthouse" of the Library Tower, the tallest building in the western United States, which stands behind it. (Courtesy of C. Roseman.)

Although a number of the larger hotels of the early 20th century were on Main Street, a few hotels of varying sizes were also built on neighboring streets. This 1905 photo shows the Angelus Hotel, which was located on the southwest corner of Fourth and Spring Streets, just one block west of Main. This hotel was razed in 1956 and replaced by a parking lot. (Courtesy of CHS.)

Even though the Baltimore Hotel is on the southwest corner of Fifth and Los Angeles Streets, one block east of Main, the lure of a Main Street address led the hotel to describe its location with reference to Main Street on this 1920s postcard. Along with numerous other hotels, both in the Historic Core and to its east, the Baltimore was used in the late 20th and early 21st centuries as a single room occupancy facility, providing affordable but usually temporary housing for the homeless and the poor. (Courtesy of C. Roseman.)

15063. Spring Street, Showing Hotel Alexandria, Los Angeles, California.

The Alexandria Hotel, seen here on a 1910s postcard, was one of a few 20th-century hotels nestled among the banks on Spring Street. Designed in 1906 by John Parkinson in partnership with Edwin Bergstrom, it is famous for its Palm Court with a stained-glass ceiling. Early in the century, the 500-room Alexandria was the highest-rated hotel in downtown Los Angeles, hosting movie stars along with three U.S. presidents, Theodore Roosevelt, William Taft, and Woodrow Wilson. (Courtesy of C. Roseman.)

One block south of the Alexandria, at Sixth and Spring Streets, is the Hayward Hotel. This 1927 photo shows two Italian Renaissance Revival additions by the John Parkinson firm, added in 1925 to the original corner building. In 2004 a large vertical neon Hayward sign was restored and relit as part of the LUMENS (Living Urban Museum of Electric and Neon Signs) project to bring back prominent neon signs in Los Angeles. (Courtesy of CHS.)

The El Rey Hotel, seen here on a 1930s postcard, was located five blocks east of Main Street, much closer to the railroad stations than the hotels on Main. Built in 1926 with 600 rooms, it became one of the largest among a major cluster of small and older hotels between the Historic Core and the Southern Pacific depots on Central Avenue—Arcade Station (18881914) and Central Station (19141939). (Courtesy of E.C. Kropp Co., Milwaukee, Wisconsin.)

Today the El Rey Building is home to the Weingart Center Association, shown in this 2004 photo. The center provides shelter and other services to over 600 homeless men and women at this skid row location. (Courtesy of C. Roseman.)

In the early 20th century the main central business district gradually moved south and west from its 19th-century core. Although most of the major hotels remained on or near Main Street north of Seventh Street, others were established outside of this area, including the Biltmore on Pershing Square in 1924. The Lankershim, pictured above in about 1907, was established in 1904 on the southwest corner of Seventh and Broadway. This intersection would reach peak real estate value in downtown Los Angeles within a few years. Remarkably, this is one of very few buildings that were razed near that intersection. This corner now hosts a modern parking structure surrounded by pre-1930 buildings. (Courtesy of CHS.)

Similar to most other American cities, no major hotels were built in the depression and war years in Los Angeles. Then came a new generation of hotels in downtown locations, the first of these being the 900-room Statler, shown in this 1950s postcard. It was built in 1951, eight blocks west of Main Street on Figueroa between Wilshire Boulevard and Seventh Street. By that time the retail sector had extended westward along Seventh Street to Figueroa and private automobile travel had clearly supplanted rail, so this location made sense for a new hotel. This area became the center of a late 20th-century hotel district, linked to the convention center a few blocks to the south and adjacent to the Harbor Freeway, and skirting the western edge of downtown Los Angeles. Established nearby were the Hyatt, the Bonaventure, the Marriott, and a couple of Holiday Inns, among others. Competition for the main-line travel and convention trade became more difficult for many hotels in the Historic Core, whose original location had been closely linked to the railroad stations to the east. In 1958 the Statler became the Statler-Hilton; later it became the Omni and the Wilshire Grand. (Courtesy of Lake County, Illinois, Discovery Museum, Curt Teich Postcard Archive.)

# *Two*

# SPRING STREET

## THE WALL STREET OF THE WEST

As the central business of downtown Los Angeles migrated to the south from its 19th-century core, an early 20th-century banking district emerged south of Third Street along Spring Street. As a result, for most of the 20th century, Spring was called the "Wall Street of the West." One by one, major banks moved to or were established along Spring Street, accompanied by a stock exchange along with a few hotels and other large business buildings. The vast majority of these buildings are still standing, especially between Third and Eighth Streets, where 30 of them are part of the Spring Street National Register Historic District.

Views of Spring Street and neighboring areas in the Historic Core reveal a uniform flat skyline, produced by the "limit height" of 150 feet, established in the early 1900s and repealed in 1957. One major exception was the 454-foot city hall built in 1928. Peeking just a bit above that 150-foot limit is Los Angeles' "first skyscraper," the Continental Building at Fourth and Spring Streets, designed by John Parkinson and completed in 1904. Today this 174-foot icon stands as an anchor for a modern 20th-century Historic Core that developed south and west of this point.

Beginning in the 1960s, the City of Los Angeles encouraged the development of a new financial district a few blocks west of Spring Street. One by one financial institutions abandoned Spring Street for modern skyscrapers in the "new downtown," several reaching heights in excess of 1,000 feet. As a result, the historic Wall Street of the West became a very quiet place in the late 20th century. At the turn of the 21st century, several of Spring Street's buildings were converted to lofts, bringing new residents to this otherwise quiet street.

This c. 1903 view of Spring Street looking north from First Street shows the La Fiesta Parade. Hundreds viewed the parade from the awning-sheltered sidewalks in front of a variety of businesses that characterized the late 19th-century downtown business core. The buildings seen here were constructed in the 1880s and 1890s, a period of rapid growth in Los Angeles. In terms of style and height these were typical of the hundreds of buildings that comprised the city's urban core. Virtually all of the buildings of this era were replaced in the 20th century by the development of the civic center, today's major center of government employment. (Courtesy of CHS.)

Another perspective on the dense 19th-century core of downtown Los Angeles, this view looks south on Spring from First Street, between 1900 and 1904. By this time an extensive trolley system connected downtown with all parts of Los Angeles. In this photo, the trolleys had to compete for space only with buggies, wagons (including the ice wagon in the lower left), and pedestrians. Soon, however, the rapid proliferation of the automobile would add considerable congestion to downtown streets. On the right is the Nadeau Hotel, which was built in 1883 on the First Street site of the current Los Angeles *Times* Building, which was completed in 1935. In the foreground on the left is the Los Angeles National Bank. The circular sign in the right foreground reads: "Up to Date Crandall Aylsworth Company Bargains." During the first three decades of the 20th century, the Wall Street of the West would develop several blocks in the distance. (Courtesy of CHS.)

The Continental Building, completed in 1904 at Fourth and Spring Streets, has rightful claims to being the first "skyscraper" in Los Angeles. At 174 feet, it was much taller than any previous building and, because of a 150-foot height limit that was imposed soon after it was completed, it remains today as the tallest of all the pre-1950s buildings in the Historic Core. Through its more than 100 year history, the Continental Building has been identified by various names, including Hibernian, California Reserve, German American Bank, and Union Trust. Originally it was the Braly Building, named after John Hyde Braly who headed the syndicate that built the building. This Los Angeles icon was designed by John Parkinson, who went on to design, or collaborate in the design of, many of the most important buildings in Los Angeles, including the Alexandria Hotel, Bullocks-Wilshire Department Store, city hall, the coliseum, and several buildings on the campus of the University of Southern California. (Courtesy of CHS.)

The Beaux-Arts–style Continental Building, the top of which is shown in this 2004 photo, has numerous decorative terracotta ornaments. Its top section, which peeks above a sea of historic buildings 24 feet shorter, has two-story arched windows separated by Corinthian columns. This was one of the first major buildings in Los Angeles to have been designed by John Parkinson, who first moved to the city in 1894. (Courtesy of G. Rein.)

This is an early photo of the Amstoy Building, built in 1888 near today's city hall, and replaced by a parking lot in 1958. On July 9, 1958, the Los Angeles *Herald-Examiner* declared the Amstoy as the city's "first skyscraper." It may have been the tallest when it was built, but within a few years numerous four- and five-story buildings were built in the 19th-century core of the city. (Courtesy of the *Examiner*.)

These facing pages illustrate the 150-foot height limit in the Historic Core. Other large American cities have had similar limits, but few resulted in extensive flat skylines. Until the 1970s, buildings in Philadelphia were limited to just under 500 feet so that none would be higher than the statue of William Penn. Washington, D.C., limits heights of building so that various national monuments will have wide visibility. The above view (c. 1917) looks westward along Sixth Street from exactly 150 feet, at the top of the Kerckhoff (now Santa Fe) Building on Main Street. In the foreground on the left (south) side of Sixth Street is the Central Building, a limit-height structure, now gone. To its west is the shorter Grosse Building (with the Occidental Life sign) that in 1959 was replaced with the only modern building on this stretch of Spring Street, the California United Bank. Across Spring Street from the Grosse Building is the Hayward Hotel. (Courtesy of CHS.)

This 2001 photo shows the flat skyline looking south along Spring Street from Sixth Street. In the right foreground is the Hayward Hotel, followed by five limit-height buildings. The first two comprise the Premier Towers, formerly the art deco E.F. Hutton Building (1931) and the California Canadian Bank (1923). Lined up farther down the street are Barclay's Bank and the Bartlett and Van Nuys Buildings. (Courtesy of C. Roseman.)

The vista in this 2001 photo shows the north side of Seventh Street centering on the Bank of America Building at the northeast corner of Seventh and Spring. Its lobby has polished marble walls and floors, vaulted ceilings, and brass teller cages. It was the headquarters for the Los Angeles Bank of America from 1930 until 1972, when the bank moved its headquarters to a skyscraper in the Financial District. The bank left the building in March 1988. (Courtesy of C. Roseman.)

Not all pre-1950s Historic Core structures conformed precisely to the 150-foot height limit. On these facing pages are three examples of buildings that significantly exceeded the limit—and did so legally so long at the spaces above 150 feet remained unoccupied. The most spectacular of these was the 338-foot-tall Atlantic Richfield Building at Fifth and Flower Streets, shown in the above 1930s photo. The imposing, art deco black and gold building, completed in 1929, justified its significant parts above the 150-foot limit as spaces devoted to a water tank and to signage. This magnificent building's relatively short life ended in 1972 when the oil company razed it for a large dual skyscraper development that soars to 699 feet above the ground and includes underground shopping and parking. (Courtesy of Whittington.)

The Texaco (later United Artists) Building is another that pierces the height limit with an unoccupied decorative tower. The top of this 1927 Spanish Gothic building is seen in this 2003 photo taken from Spring Street between Eighth and Ninth Streets. (Courtesy of C. Roseman.)

The Title Guarantee Building at Fifth and Hill Streets has another of the decorative building tops that exceeded the 150-foot height limit at 225 feet. Completed in 1931 by John and Donald Parkinson, this art deco gem, located at Fifth and Hill Streets, is seen against a backdrop of Financial District skyscrapers. (Courtesy of C. Roseman.)

The original Farmers and Merchants Bank on Main and Commercial Streets, shown here in 1895, was located just north of today's city hall in the 19th-century downtown core. Founded in 1871, Farmers and Merchants was the first incorporated bank in Los Angeles. Its president, Isaias W. Hellman, remained in that position until 1920. (Courtesy of CHS.)

This newer Farmers and Merchants Bank was built on Main Street in 1905 just east of the Continental Building on Fourth Street. The Classic Revival style of this building, shown here c. 1908, contrasts with the larger bank buildings on Spring, most of which were designed in Beaux-Arts or other styles popular in the early 20th century. (Courtesy of CHS.)

This *c.* 1923 view shows the neighborhood of the Farmers and Merchants Bank between Main and Spring Streets along Fourth Street. Surrounding the 1905 bank is an office building built by and named after the bank's president, Isaias W. Hellman. In the background is Los Angeles's "first skyscraper," the Continental Building on Spring Street, at that time called the Hibernian Building (viewed from its less flattering east perspective). In the early 2000s these three buildings became part of a pioneering residential loft development called the "Old Bank District." Subsequently, loft developments would spread to numerous other buildings in the Historic Core. Beyond the Continental Building across Spring Street is the Angelus Hotel. In the right foreground is the Van Nuys Hotel, which was completed nine years before the bank building. (Courtesy of CHS.)

The 1928 Los Angeles City Hall is shown in the distance in this early 1950s photo looking north from Fourth and Spring Streets. Dramatically taller than any other building at 454 feet, it instantly became a central visual icon for Los Angeles, shining above an otherwise flat skyline until after the 150-foot height limit was lifted in 1957. Los Angeles City Hall became the centerpiece of the large civic center that replaced the old 19th-century downtown core. City, county, state, and federal buildings, along with associated plazas, came to dominate that area by the middle of the 20th century. In the left foreground is the Angelus Hotel, which was replaced by a parking lot in 1956. Trolley tracks are still visible in this photo, although most of the street railways ceased to operate in the early 1950s. The Pontiacs, Fords, Cadillacs, and other rubber-tired vehicles now had the streets to themselves. (Courtesy of CHS.)

This 1929 photo, taken from roughly the same location as the previous one, also shows Los Angeles City Hall in the background. On the right is the building that the city hall replaced in 1928 as the tallest in Los Angeles, the 174-foot Continental Building, which at the time of the photo was called California Reserve Building. John Parkinson, who designed the Continental Building in 1904, also participated in the design of city hall and, indeed, in the design of over 40 buildings in the Historic Core. Just beyond the Continental Building is the 1903 Beaux-Arts Herman W. Hellman Building, known after 1974 as Banco Popular. Herman was the brother of Isaias W. Hellman, president of the Farmers and Merchants Bank just around the corner on Main Street. In the right foreground is the Stowell Hotel, later called the El Dorado, a 1913 building with a Neo-Gothic facade. (Courtesy of the *Examiner.*)

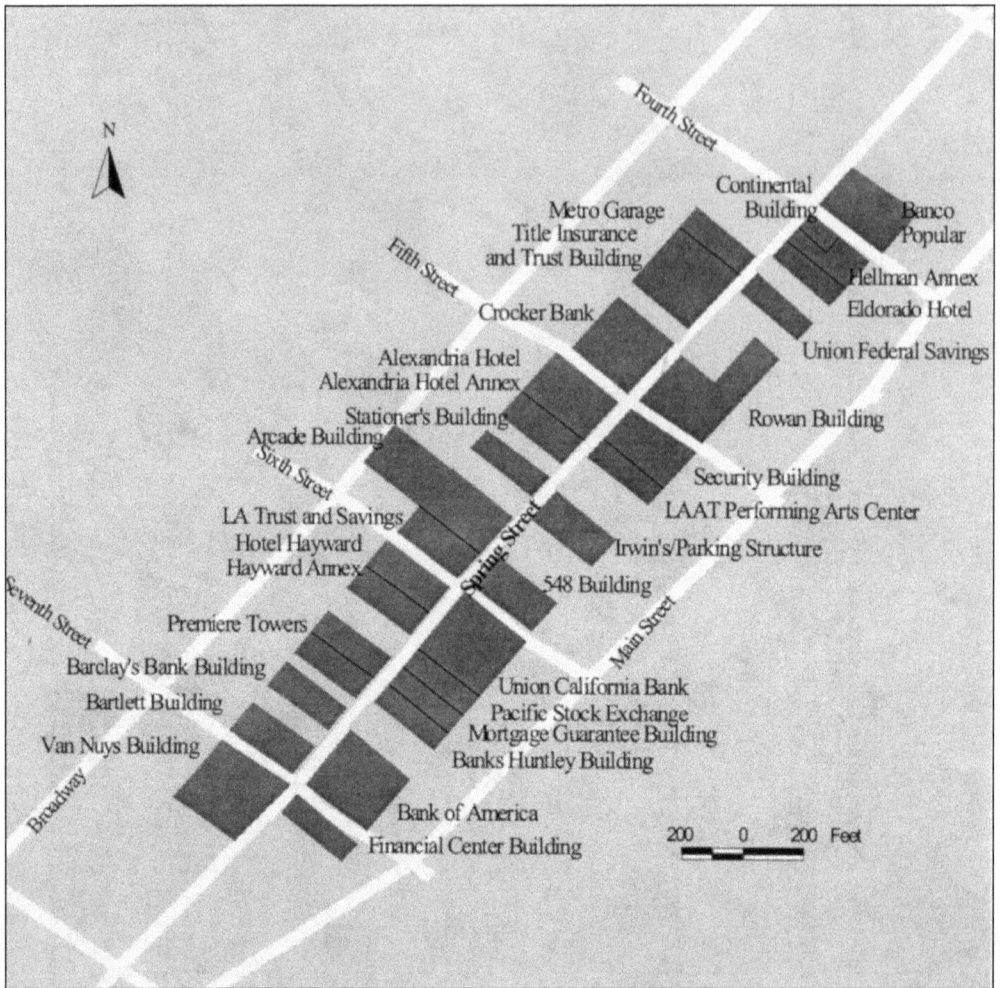

The development of the 20th-century Wall Street of the West resulted in a significant cluster of historic buildings along Spring Street. In 1979 this three-block area, which encompasses 31 buildings, was recognized as the Spring Street National Register Historic District. The historic buildings in the district range in age from the 1903 Beaux-Arts Banco Popular Building to the 1931 art deco Banks Huntley Building, and most push right up to the limit height. An exception is the First Interstate Building, a taller modern structure completed in 1959. Architect John Parkinson designed or participated in the design of 15 of the buildings in this historic district. (Courtesy of G. DeVerteuil.)

The Metro Garage Building at 417 South Spring, shown here in 1952, was built next to the Angelus Hotel. By the 1920s American central business districts began making significant accommodations for the automobile, building parking structures and lots. Indeed, in 1956, the Angelus was replaced by a parking lot. The Metro Garage Building later became part of the Los Angeles Design Center with its neighbor to the south (left in this photo), the Title Insurance and Trust Company Building. (Courtesy of the *Examiner*.)

The Title Insurance and Trust Company Building at 433 South Spring was designed by John Parkinson and completed in 1928. Shown in this late 1920s photo, this Art Deco office building, along with its neighbor on the right (north), later became the Los Angeles Design Center. (Courtesy of Whittington.)

49

John Parkinson and Edwin Bergstrom designed the Security Trust and Savings Bank and office building at Fifth and Spring Streets. This 1926 photo shows the office building frontage on Fifth Street with the Alexandria Hotel across Spring Street in the background. In 1985 the bank became the Los Angeles Theater Center, a facility with four theaters. (Courtesy of CHS.)

This 1910 photo shows both older and newer buildings as Spring Street was in the process of developing into the Wall Street of the West. In the foreground is the All Night And Day Bank at the northeast corner of Sixth and Spring. In the background are two early limit-height buildings, the Security Building to the left and the Kerckhoff Building on Main on the far right, indicators of what was to come on Spring Street. (Courtesy of CHS.)

The Grosse Building, across the street at the southeast corner of Sixth and Spring Streets, was the headquarters for the Southern Pacific Railroad. It is shown in this c. 1908 photo with the Central and the Pacific Electric Buildings on Main Street in the background. (Courtesy of CHS.)

In 1959 the Grosse Building was replaced by the United California Bank (later First Interstate Bank), which pierced the newly lifted height limit by several stories and replaced the Continental Building as the tallest on Spring Street. Because of its height and its modern style, the new bank building looks out of place on this stretch of Spring Street. (Courtesy of Whittington.)

The graceful Los Angeles Trust and Savings Bank, designed by John Parkinson, rose at the northwest corner of Sixth and Spring Streets in 1910. Seen in the far left background of this c. 1915 photo is the back of the First Methodist Episcopal Church on Pershing Square. (Courtesy of CHS.)

The Los Angeles Trust and Savings Building would get bigger and become the Pacific Southwest Building by the time of this 1930s photo, when it housed the Security First National Bank. The photo also shows the Arcade Building to the right (north) with one of its two old radio towers sporting the famous call-sign KRKD. (Courtesy of Whittington.)

By the mid-1920s the basic form of the 20th-century Wall Street of the West had been established, as can be seen in this 1924 view north on Spring Street from about Sixth Street. In the left foreground are the Hayward Hotel and the Los Angeles Trust and Savings Building, both on the corner of Sixth Street. Beyond them are the Arcade Building and the Alexandria Hotel. In the right foreground are the Grosse Building and the 1915 Merchants National Bank Building, which later became Lloyds Bank. Beyond that is the Security Building at the corner of Fifth Street, and in the distance is the Continental Building at the corner of Fourth Street. Trolleys, automobiles, and pedestrians all shared street space in the 1920s. As a result, the downtown streets of Los Angeles—especially at rush hour—were extremely congested. (Courtesy of CHS.)

Shown in this 1920 photo is the Stock Exchange Building at 639 South Spring Street, which was the seventh home to the Los Angeles Stock Exchange. The exchange would move across the street in 1931 to its eighth home in a new building. (Courtesy of the *Examiner.*)

The Los Angeles Stock Exchange, completed in 1931, was one of the last buildings to be built in the Historic Core. Designed by Samuel E. Lunden, this Classic Moderne building includes a taller tower in the rear, as shown in this 1920s drawing. (Courtesy of Whittington.)

This 1940s photo shows the completed Los Angeles Stock Exchange Building. In 1957 this institution merged with the San Francisco Stock Exchange to become the Pacific Coast Stock Exchange. In 1973 it changed its name to the Pacific Stock Exchange. (Courtesy of Whittington.)

This photo shows an interior view of the 1931 Los Angeles Stock Exchange Building. In the late 1980s the exchange was moved to new headquarters west of the Harbor Freeway, the last major financial institution to leave Spring Street. One by one from the 1960s through the 1980s, banks abandoned their old buildings here for sleek new facilities in the tall towers of the financial district a few blocks west. (Courtesy of CHS.)

This 1930s photo shows the Los Angeles Stock Exchange nestled amongst bank and office buildings on the east side of Spring between Sixth and Seventh Streets. Note the well-marked trolley waiting areas on the street. Note also the style of street lamps that have been maintained or brought back to many areas of downtown Los Angeles. (Courtesy of CHS.)

This photo, looking north on Spring Street in 1959, shows the Pacific Coast Stock Exchange with old and new neighbors. Beyond the exchange is the modern California Bank Building. On this side of the exchange are the Mortgage Guarantee Building and the art deco Banks Huntley Building. In the right foreground is the Bank of America Building. (Courtesy of Whittington.)

At the time of this 1926 photo, the northwest corner of Seventh and Spring Streets was home to the Beaux-Arts A. G. Bartlett Building, which was designed by John Parkinson and Edwin Bergstrom and completed in 1911. It has also been known as the Union Oil Building, and housed the Security Trust and Savings Bank. (Courtesy of CHS.)

This view of the northwest corner of Seventh and Spring is nearly identical to the 1926 view in the previous photo, but taken 20 years earlier. Before the 20th-century "Wall Street" invasion, this section of Spring Street was low density and included residences. Trolley tracks were in place but the street was not yet paved. (Courtesy of CHS.)

The Victorian residence of Isaac Newton Van Nuys at Seventh and Spring Streets provides the backdrop for this c. 1902 photo of a man driving a horseless carriage. Just ten years later the large Beaux-Arts I.N. Van Nuys Building was constructed at the southwest corner of this intersection. (Courtesy of CHS.)

This 1905 photo looks south on Spring from Seventh Street. The Wall Street of the West had not yet arrived this far south on Spring Street, which at the time remained unpaved. In the background is the Armory Building on Eighth Street. (Courtesy of CHS.)

The Armory Building at the northwest corner of Eighth and Spring Streets is shown in this c. 1908 photo. Among the businesses that occupied this building were the *Evening News* and Vance's Drug Store. Residences are on either side of the armory, and the four-year-old Lankershim Hotel on Seventh and Broadway can be seen in the distance. (Courtesy of CHS.)

About 16 years later, the northwest corner of Eighth and Spring Streets looked like this. Today the Wall Street of the West surrounds the Armory Building. This c. 1924 view shows larger buildings on each of the other three corners of the intersection, the Van Nuys Building behind the Armory on Seventh Street, and downtown street congestion typical of the 1920s. (Courtesy of CHS.)

In the early 20th century, one or more shopping arcades were built inside downtown buildings in most large American cities and in numerous cities elsewhere in the world. Shown in this 2004 photo is the Spring Street side of the Arcade Building, which extends from Spring to Broadway. The lower floors of the 1923 limit-height building are of Spanish Renaissance design. (Courtesy of C. Roseman.)

The magnificent portal of the Arcade Building leads to the interior shopping arcade that features balconies and a skylight. Like many other buildings in the Historic Core, the Arcade Building was converted to lofts in the early 2000s. (Courtesy of C. Roseman.)

# *Three*

# BROADWAY
## THE GREAT WHITE WAY

Broadway Street has showcased many of the city's theaters and stores since the early years of the 20th century. Illuminated with a blaze of electric lights and vibrant theater life, the moniker is as fitting as it is for New York's famous avenue. From Second to Tenth Streets Broadway offered Los Angelinos a heady mix of vaudeville and cinema in beautiful theater houses and shopping in stately department stores. Most of these majestic buildings still stand; indeed, Broadway has the largest concentration of historic theaters in the nation. Although the large department stores have either moved or closed, their buildings remain as icons of an earlier era.

Around the turn of the 20th century the city's center, the plaza, began to outgrow its compact amalgam of shops, churches, and residences, and businesses began migrating south along Main, Spring, and Broadway. Those early years saw a frenzy of theater construction on Broadway, with the opening of each theater heralded by the local newspapers. From 1903 until 1930 at least 19 theaters were built. Meanwhile, the *grande dames* of retail, the department stores, positioned themselves strategically on Broadway's corners, the first being the fittingly named Broadway Department Store. Soon to follow were Hamburger's People's Store (later the May Company) and Bullocks. Complementing them was a host of smaller variety stores and specialty shops. Sprinkled among the retail businesses were several buildings that are now historic landmarks, such as the Bradbury, the Eastern Columbia, and the Broadway Arcade. The history of Broadway has not been limited to retail and entertainment enterprises, as the newspaper industry also flourished there. Buildings owned by two of the more prominent newspapers, the Los Angeles *Times* and the Los Angeles *Examiner*, anchored both ends of the street over several decades.

In contrast to the early heyday years when railway lines brought shoppers and theatergoers to the city and to Broadway, the 1920s marked the beginning of a reverse migration. The growing suburbs and the convenience of automobile travel spurred businesses to develop away from downtown. Theaters began moving to Hollywood, an emerging entertainment center, and department stores opened branches in outlying areas. In 1929 Bullocks opened a new store with a parking lot, and by 1941 almost all of the major department stores had branches in the suburbs. A new revitalization period begun in the 1950s eventually created a new Broadway. Although not all of the historic buildings function in their former capacity today, their presence recalls the early Broadway, which now pulses with an energetic Latino flavor. Theater marquees and retail stores display Spanish-language advertising, and the air is filled with aromas of exotic cuisine and the rhythms of salsa and mariachi music.

In 1906 Broadway bustled with pedestrians, trolleys, horse buggies, and even a few automobiles, their occupants drawn to the stores and other businesses that lined both sides of the street. Visible in the distance, the second city hall stands at the northern end of the street, as if marking the starting point for this rapidly developing business district. The Broadway Central Building and Parmelee-Dohrman Company rise above their neighbors and declare their presence with bold advertising. These tall buildings, as well as the Belasco Theater seen in the right-hand corner, hint at Broadway's future role as the focal retail and entertainment thoroughfare of Los Angeles. (Courtesy of CHS.)

This undated view of Los Angeles City Hall at Second and Broadway may have been taken soon after it was built in 1888, for it shows a street with a residential look and no evidence of the multi-storied structures soon to come. This Romanesque style building is a contrast to the city's first city hall, a one-story adobe building in the plaza. (Courtesy of CHS.)

The Bradbury Building at Third and Broadway is the oldest commercial building remaining in downtown Los Angeles and one of its most unique. In 1893 designer George Wyman created a building with a fairly modest exterior that belied its dramatic interior courtyard, with its open cage elevators, marble stairs, and ornate iron railings. This 1961 view looks straight up to the skylight from the courtyard. (Courtesy of the *Examiner*.)

This 1985 mural of Mexican-born actor Anthony Quinn by Eloy Torrez is one of several commissioned by the Victor Clothing Company to honor its Spanish-speaking employees and customers. The company, established in 1920 at 242 South Broadway, served the community for eight decades. The photograph dates from 1998. (Courtesy of R. Wallach.)

In 1886 Harrison Gray Otis, the new owner and publisher of the Los Angeles *Times*, moved the newspaper from the Downey Block to First and Broadway, then known as Fort Street. At that time the average daily circulation for the paper was approximately 8,000. This 1886 view shows a solid Romanesque brick building bordered by a yet unpaved street. (Courtesy of CHS.)

During the time of Harrison Gray Otis's ownership, the Los Angeles *Times* editorials and employee relations reflected his staunchly conservative and anti-union views. On October 1, 1910, during a strike called to unionize different trade workers, the *Times* building was destroyed by dynamite. Two unionist brothers, James B. and John J. McNamara, were eventually brought to trial and found guilty of the bombing. (Courtesy of CHS.)

After the bombing of its Broadway building in 1910 the Los Angeles *Times* moved to Spring Street. In 1935 the paper moved to new headquarters at 123 South Spring Street, where it still resides. The building's Streamline Moderne style, designed by Gordon B. Kaufmann, won a gold medal at the 1937 Paris Exposition. (Courtesy of Whittington.)

In 1903 William Randolph Hearst established the Los Angeles *Examiner* newspaper as a voice for the city's progressive community. The first headquarters were at 509–511 South Broadway, shown in this 1906 view. The modest six-story building is adorned by a decidedly commanding facsimile of the *Examiner* name on the roof and over the front entrance. (Courtesy of CHS.)

By 1913 the Los Angeles *Examiner* had outgrown its Fifth and Broadway location and moved to the southern end of Broadway at Eleventh Street. Julia Morgan, one of America's leading women architects, designed the new headquarters in a Spanish Renaissance style, conforming to William Randolph Hearst's desire for a building that reflected the romance and history of Southern California. (Courtesy of Whittington.)

This 1934 Labor Day parade winds it way up Broadway past the Los Angeles *Examiner* building. When it merged with the *Herald-Express* in 1962 to form a new evening newspaper, the Los Angeles *Herald-Examiner*, the headquarters remained at Eleventh and Broadway. In 1989 the newspaper met its demise and since then the building has housed various tenants and been targeted for various future projects. (Courtesy of the *Examiner*.)

In this July 1903 view automobiles are lined up for a parade, perhaps in celebration of the Fourth of July. This was a novel and light-hearted use of what would become a cultural and transportation phenomenon, eventually dominating the landscape of Southern California. (Courtesy of CHS.)

La Fiesta de Los Angeles was first held in 1894 to celebrate the city's Hispanic heritage and to attract tourists. The festival of parades, floral battles in Central Park (Pershing Square), a grand ball, and fireworks was an annual event for ten years. This 1901 view shows that year's chamber of commerce parade entry. Over the decades the event was revived in different configurations and today lives on as L.A. Fiesta Broadway. (Courtesy of CHS.)

The Mason Opera House was Los Angeles's "old op'ry house" during the early years of the 20th century. In 1903 John Mason, a descendant of an old Spanish family, sought to rival Child's Grand Opera House on Main Street and opened his showplace at 127 South Broadway with a production of *If I Were King*. His venture was a success and the house continued to draw crowds for many years to its theater and light opera productions. Lillian Russell, Maude Adams, Dustin Farnum, and Ethel Barrymore were among the many who graced the stage of the Mason. During the 1920s, 1930s, and 1940s the theater's popularity waned and peaked with various attempts to recapture the glory of the early years. For a brief period in the late 1930s the theater was renamed "Teatro Mason" and showcased Spanish vaudeville and films from Mexico. In the 1940s a more cosmopolitan fare was offered. Nevertheless, the Mason could not compete with the larger palatial theaters and in 1954 its doors closed after the final production, a Mexican film entitled *Pueblerina*. The theater was razed in 1956. (Courtesy of CHS.)

Tally's Theater at 833 South Broadway was built in 1910. Although it gained fame as the first theater to house a pipe organ and an elevated orchestra pit, it did not flourish as well as the larger and more palatial theaters and succumbed to the wrecker's ball in 1929. (Courtesy of the *Examiner*.)

The Cameo Theater at 528 South Broadway, designed by Alfred F. Rosenheim, was built in 1910 by early film impresario William H. "Billy" Clune. The theater closed in 1991, making it one of the longest operating movie theaters in California. Its close neighbor, the Roxie, was built much later in 1932, one of the last opulent movie theaters to be erected in Los Angeles, and unique for its art deco style. (Courtesy of Whittington.)

Chorus girls practice their steps on the roof of the Palace Theater in this photo from 1928. The Palace Theater, just south of Sixth Street on Broadway, was the third home of the Orpheum vaudeville circuit. Built in 1926, it is the oldest remaining Orpheum theater in the United States. (Courtesy of Whittington.)

Loew's State Theater at Seventh Street and Broadway was built by film mogul Marcus Loew in 1921. The Spanish Renaissance building was the largest of the movie palaces, with 2,450 seats, and offered both film and vaudeville. In 1929 Judy Garland appeared there as one of the "Singing Gumm Sisters." The theater now functions as a church and is also occasionally used for movie productions. (Courtesy of the *Examiner*.)

The first motion picture house on Broadway, the Million Dollar Theater, seen here in a 1920s postcard, was built on the intersection with Third Street in 1918 by showman Sid Grauman. In the 1950s it became the premier venue for Spanish-language films and variety shows known as "variedades." After a period of decline the theater reopened in 1999 for various kinds of events. (Courtesy of C. Roseman.)

The Tower Theater at Eighth and Broadway was built on an unbelievably narrow lot of 50 feet, yet the ingenious design by S. Charles Lee accommodates 1,000 seats. It features a landmark tower blending Spanish Baroque, Moorish, and French Renaissance architectural styles. This 1928 view was taken a year after the theater opened with the world premier of Warner Brothers's *The Jazz Singer*, the first film with synchronized sound. (Courtesy of CHS.)

The Orpheum Theater at 842 South Broadway was built in 1926 and was the fourth and last of the Orpheum vaudeville circuit. Featured acts included Eddie Cantor, Sophie Tucker, Will Rogers, Lena Horne, Bob Hope, and Jack Benny. In 1928 a great Wurlitzer organ was installed to provide music for the vaudeville acts and later for film. This 1939 oblique view shows architectural features which hint at the theater's interior splendor. (Courtesy of Whittington.)

The movie *Cimarron* premiered at the Orpheum Theater in 1931. Based on the novel by Edna Ferber, the film was directed by Wesley Ruggles, written by Edna Ferber and Howard Estabrook, and starred Richard Dix, Irene Dunne, and Estelle Taylor. The gala premier was followed by parties at the Roosevelt Hotel in Hollywood. The following day newspapers reported who was there and what they wore to the premier. (Courtesy of Whittington.)

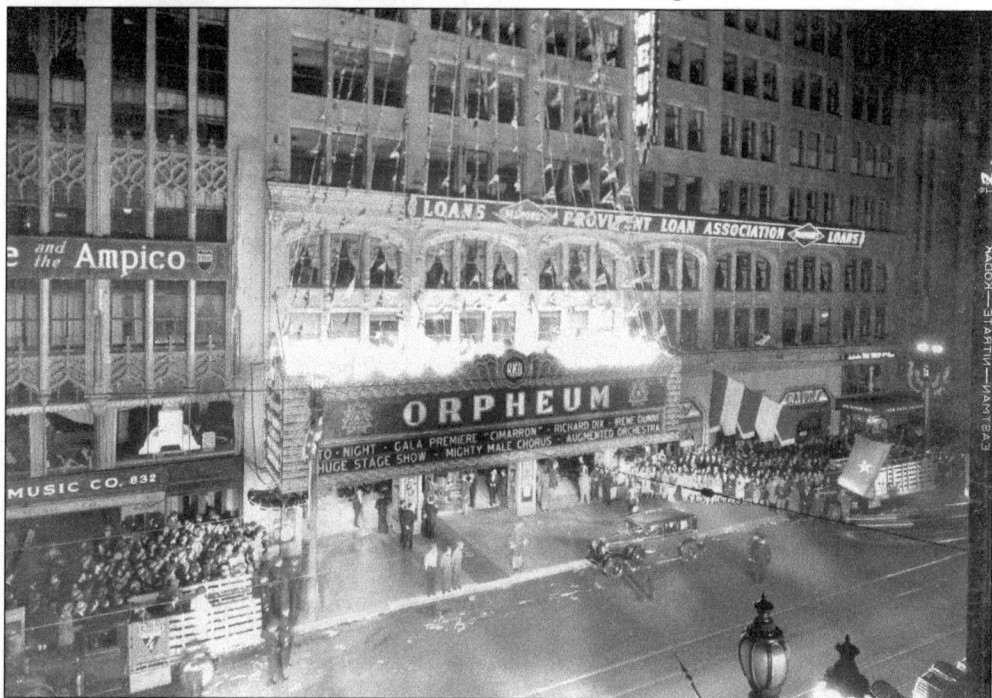

The United Artists Theater at 933 South Broadway anchors the southern end of the Broadway Theater District. Built in 1927, it was the crown jewel of the United Artist Theater Circuit, a venture formed in 1919 by D.W. Griffith, Charlie Chaplin, Mary Pickford, and Douglas Fairbanks. Its Spanish Gothic style, as seen in this 1928 view, made it unique among its sister theaters. (Courtesy of Whittington.)

How could the United Artists Theater not meet success, when promoted by shrewd financial supporters and some of the most famous personalities of cinema? Shown here from left to right are I.W. Freud, John Barrymore, Mary Pickford, Douglas Fairbanks, and D.W. Griffith beckoning audiences to the opening. The feature film was My Best Girl, starring Mary Pickford. (Courtesy of the Examiner.)

The Los Angeles Theater at Sixth and Broadway was designed by S. Charles Lee for H.L. Gumbiner, entrepreneur and film exhibitor. It was the last, and perhaps the finest, of the great movie palaces to be built on Broadway. The theater's $1 million plus cost was reflected in the opulence of its French Baroque style. The central notched arch is framed by Corinthian columns. Inside, the majestic lobby's architectural details recall the splendors of Versailles. A three-tiered fountain, crystal chandeliers, gilt ornaments, fluted marble columns, and a grand central staircase are enhanced by walls of mirrors. In addition to the two-story theater space, the building's grandeur is extended to a restaurant and glass-ceiling ballroom. The theater opened in 1931 with a gala premier of Charlie Chaplin's *City Lights*. The Los Angeles is among several theaters that in recent years have been used occasionally for fund-raising events. (Courtesy of Whittington.)

This view shows the Los Angeles Theater's two-story main theater. The luxuriant decorative style is evident in columns topped with sculptures, ornate ceiling adornments, and richly decorated curtains. (Courtesy of CHS.)

A few years before the last of the palatial Broadway theaters was built, Los Angeles gained a new city hall, and in 1928 its dedication was celebrated with the appropriate festivities. This view taken from the chamber of commerce building shows a parade winding its way down Broadway. (Courtesy of CHS.)

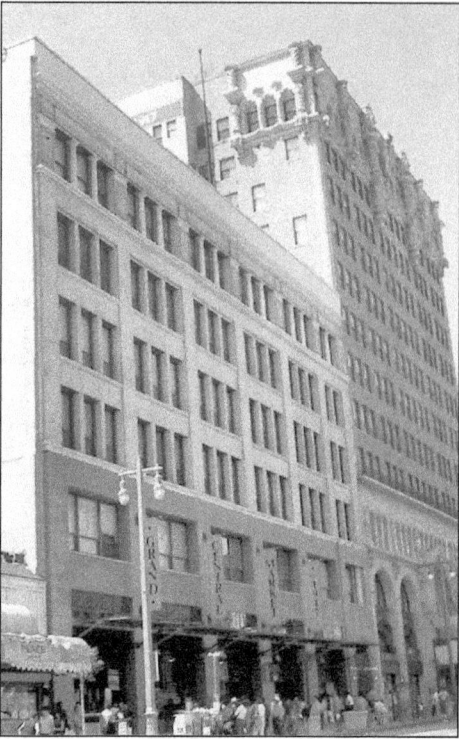

One of the earliest shopping establishments on Broadway was the Homer Laughlin Building at 315 South Broadway. Designed by L.A. Parkinson and built in 1897, it has been home to various firms, including Grand Central Market, which took up residence on the ground floor in 1917. Seen in this 2004 photo, the market has over 50 privately owned vending stalls, drawing regular shoppers and flocks of tourists. (Courtesy of L. McCann.)

The first Broadway Department Store, on the corner of Fourth and Broadway, was built in 1896 by Arthur Letts. In 1903 more than 30,000 people visited the store to view the new spring fashions, a remarkable turnout for a city with a population of 130,000. (Courtesy of CHS.)

The new Broadway Department Store, a Beaux-Arts design by the L.A. Parkinson firm, was built in 1914 at the same location as its predecessor. It was nine stories high, had 14 passenger elevators and such amenities as a café, an auditorium, and a nursery. In 1995 the building was purchased jointly by the state and the city to provide space for more than 30 state offices. (Courtesy of Whittington.)

In November 1955 several hundred orphans were the guests of the Broadway Department Store. The Los Angeles *Examiner* reported that the children were treated to a preview of Christmas Toyland and fun and games with Goo-Goo the clown. (Courtesy of the *Examiner*.)

This view shows Bullock's Department Store under construction in 1906 at the corner of Seventh and Broadway, formerly the site of St. Vincent's College. The builder was retail magnate Arthur Letts, who also built the Broadway Department Store. (Courtesy of CHS.)

When Bullock's Department Store opened in 1907 Arthur Letts named it after its manager, John Bullock. At that time it was one of the largest commercial establishments in the city and the first to introduce escalators. This 1950 view shows the understated exterior beauty of the building. It currently houses the jewelry business St. Vincent's Galleria. (Courtesy of Whittington.)

Hamburger's People's Store at Eighth Street and Broadway, built in 1906, was designed by Alfred F. Rosenheim in the Beaux-Arts style. Hamburger's was the first large department store in downtown Los Angeles. In 1929 ownership changed and the store was renamed the May Company. (*Courtesy of* the *Examiner.*)

In 1929 the former Hamburger's People's Store became the May Company. A few decades later the store followed the trend of its sister department stores and branched out to the growing suburbs. In the mid-1980s the downtown store relocated to Seventh Street and in 1993 merged with Robinson's Department Store. Currently the building is known as the Broadway Trade Center. (Courtesy of Whittington.)

In 1954 the downtown department stores were still major retail centers, and sales drew large crowds, as evidenced by the bustle in the May Company basement. That year the annual "Sale of Sales" attracted thousands of bargain hunters, exceeding the previous year's totals. (Courtesy of the *Examiner*.)

In 1958 the Dodgers moved from Brooklyn to Los Angeles, a memorable event in baseball history. On April 1919th the new team was greeted by dignitaries, politicians, film stars, and enthusiastic crowds along the parade route. Pretty May Company employees displaying civic pride prompted the Los Angeles *Examiner* to exclaim, "Pulchritude Comes out to Root for the Club." (Courtesy of the *Examiner*.)

The Eastern Columbia Building at 849 South Broadway is one of the finest examples of the art deco Moderne style remaining in downtown Los Angeles. Designed by Claude Beelman in 1930, it was built as the new headquarters for two clothing stores, the Eastern Outfitting Company and the Columbia Outfitting Company. The 13-story structure is built of steel reinforced concrete and has a striking turquoise, green, and gold terracotta exterior. Geometric shapes, sunburst patterns, zigzags, chevrons, stylized animal and plant forms decorate the facade. Deeply recessed windows between columns impose strong vertical lines rising to the four-sided clock tower. The sidewalks surrounding the building are of multi-colored terrazzo laid in geometric patterns. (Courtesy of Whittington.)

This 1938 view taken from the Loew's Theater building shows the quintessential Broadway, a mix of entertainment and retail, housed in architectural splendor. The aerial perspective shows how the flow of humans and vehicles is conducted by well-defined traffic lanes, islands for trolley passengers, curbside parking areas, and pedestrian crosswalks. On the left side of the street is a partial view of the Bullock's Department Store roof. On the right can be seen the Palace Theater, whose name aptly reflects its opulence. Adjacent to the Palace are retail establishments, including some of the city's most elegant clothiers, such as Brooks and Desmond's, the latter one of the first men's clothing chains in the city. Farther north is the Beaux-Arts–style Walter P. Story and Garage Building. The Broadway Arcade Building, just north of Sixth Street, extends through to Spring Street, and is topped by one of two radio station KRKD towers. In the distance, city hall rises above the Broadway skyline. (Courtesy of Whittington.)

# FOUR

# HILL STREET
## THE CITY SPILLS OVER

In the Mexican era, Hill Street was called *Calle de Toros*, the Street of the Bulls, and was a site for bullfights. After California joined the Union in 1850, Hill Street developed, during the latter part of the 19th century as a mixed residential and commercial street. At the turn of the 20th century, Hill Street became increasingly commercial just south of the intersection with Fifth Street. As the city grew in the early part of the 20th century, businesses spilled over from Broadway and Spring Streets, pushing residential areas west, so that by the 1930s Hill Street was a locus for a variety of commercial activities, from drug stores and small hotels, to clothing stores and movie theaters. Unlike the other streets of the Historic Core, Hill Street didn't have a particular identity. By the 1920s automobile traffic north of Sixth Street increased substantially, warranting plans for widening the street and extending it farther north into today's Chinatown. The latter happened only in the 1960s, but already by 1940 Hill Street had become so congested, the Los Angeles *Examiner* reported, that only "radical reorganization" could enable it to be of continued service. From the 1910s into the 1950s, Hill Street accommodated four rail lines, eight bus lines, and 16,500 automobiles carrying in excess of 75,000 persons per day. From the 1930s onward, members of the Central Business District Association felt that mass transit hindered automobile traffic, a belief that eventually played into the decision by the city to dismantle its trolley system in the 1950s. After World War II, Hill Street suffered economic decline (as was true for much of the Historic Core), as commercial and residential activities moved out of the downtown area. Nevertheless, when the civic center was expanding west in 1955, Hill Street went through another important transformation. Its landmark tunnel between First and Temple Streets, atop which lay "one of the finest pioneer residential sections," was demolished to allow for the expansion, the street was resurfaced, and its streetcar tracks removed.

Since the 1970s, Hill Street between Fifth and Seventh has become the locus of the city's jewelry trade, which is centered in the International Jewelry Center, a 16-story building facing Pershing Square on Sixth and Hill Streets. The jewelry industry in Los Angeles, while nationally significant, is composed mostly of small firms and is of a varied ethnic mix. Many of the owners are Armenian, Jewish, Asian, Hispanic, or Arab, with a large majority born outside of the United States. A large percentage of workers in the industry are Hispanic and Asian, and over a third are female. This chapter moves through Hill Street in time, showing its development from a mostly residential street to a largely commercial one. Today, the historic part of Hill Street is anchored by the Fort Moore Pioneer Memorial and county government buildings to the north, with Central Market, Angels Flight, and the Jewelry District in the middle, and a variety of commercial endeavors to the south.

This photograph shows the exterior of Fort Moore, topped by a squat clock tower, looking northeast from First and Hill Streets, c. 1875. The fort was decommissioned in 1853 but remained a fixture of Los Angeles into the early 20th century. Sonoratown (the Mexican downtown residential neighborhood) is in the background. The city's first high school can be seen in Sonoratown to the right. (Courtesy of CHS.)

The Fort Moore Pioneer Memorial just above Hill Street, seen here in a 2004 photo, was dedicated on July 3, 1957. It commemorates the fort completed by the Mormon Battalion of the U.S. Army in 1847. The original fort was named in memory of Captain Benjamin Davies Moore, who was one of 21 Americans killed during the battle of San Pasqual near San Diego in December 1846. Though this battle, the largest in California during the Mexican-American War, was a military victory for the Californians led by Andres Pico, it failed to stop American forces from capturing Los Angeles a month later. (Courtesy of R. Wallach.)

The second Los Angeles high school, Fort Moore Hill, is shown here in 1908. Los Angeles's first high school was located at what was then called Poundcake Hill, near First and Broadway. In 1873 it moved to Fort Moore Hill and in 1917 moved to its current location on Olympic Boulevard and Rimpau Avenue. (Courtesy of CHS.)

This view of Hill Street looking south from Court Street shows an unpaved street and large residences, c.— 1886. Court Street, no longer extant, is briefly described on the following page. (Courtesy of CHS.)

The Bradbury mansion on Hill and Court Streets, shown here c. 1890, was the home of John Bradbury, son of the builder of the Bradbury Building. It was razed in 1929. Court Street was the only east-west street in the northern section of Bunker Hill (between Temple and First Streets) and was not familiar to many, except for its residents, since it was sealed off between Flower and Hill Streets. Court Street was once known as a mellow, old-fashioned, tree-lined neighborhood with many quaint frame homes. One of the city's jails was also on Court Street, and in the 19th century it would occasionally be invaded by the curious witnessing a hanging. In addition, Court Street had a small funicular railway, similar to Angels Flight, called Court Flight. (Courtesy of CHS.)

This view of Hill Street looks north at Second Street during the 1930s. The Hill Street Tunnel shown here was demolished in the 1950s during the expansion of the civic center. The offices of the *Southwest Builder and Contractor*, an important publication for building and engineering practitioners, can be seen on the right. (Courtesy of Whittington.)

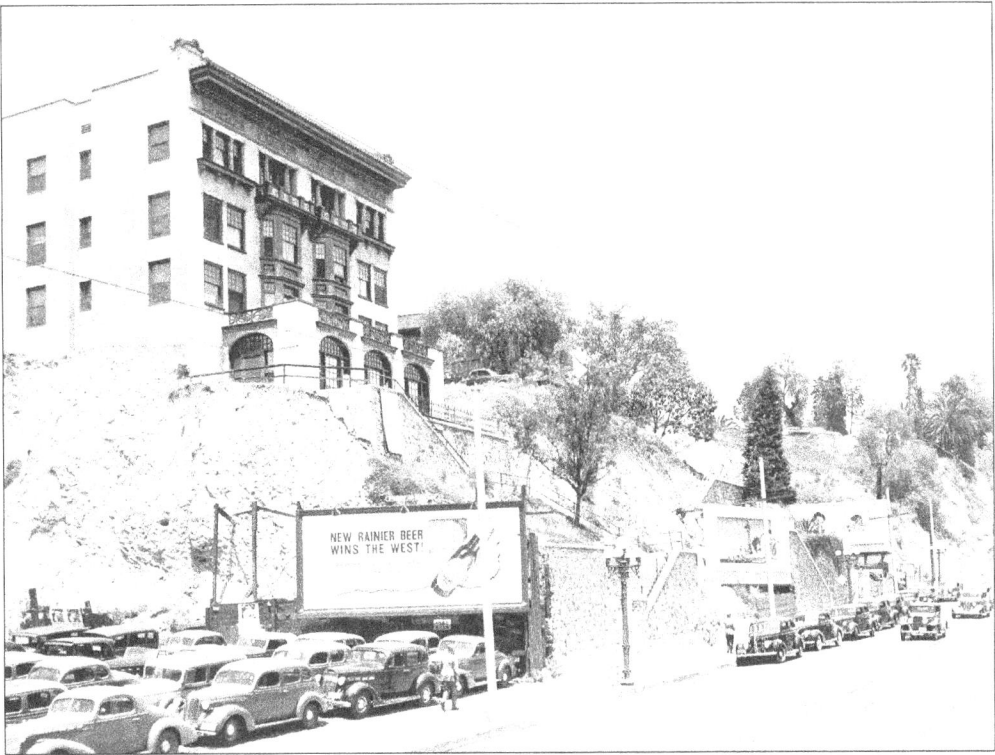

Hotel Moore Cliff, just north of Second Street, was one of the more modest hotels dotting Hill Street. As seen here in the 1930s, it advertised well-furnished modern rooms for $3 per week. A banner hanging in front of the stairwell leading to the hotel says: "Hot water, steam heat, inspection invited." (Courtesy of Whittington.)

This image from the early 1890s shows Hill Street as seen from the intersection of Olive and Third Streets on Bunker Hill. The second city hall, located on Broadway, is the building at the right with the tall, square tower. This residential part of Hill Street is lined with two-story Victorian and California bungalows. (Courtesy of CHS.)

Angels Flight, as seen at the Hill Street Tunnel in this 1907 photograph, was the shortest paying railway in the world. Its two cable cars, Olivet and Sinai, carried residents to the fashionable Victorian neighborhood on Bunker Hill. In 1901 Col. James Ward Eddy (1832–1914) was granted a 30-year franchise to Angels Flight, which he operated until 1912. After Eddy sold the railway to Funding Company of Los Angeles, it went through several additional sales, and was dismantled in 1969 during the redevelopment of the massive California Plaza office complex. The funicular was restored under a contract with the Los Angeles Conservancy and reopened in 1996. During this period of horse-drawn carriages, drivers could receive a $100 fine for "riding driving or propelling in any vehicle faster than eight (8) miles per hour" in the tunnel. Note the vegetarian restaurant next to the stairwell leading to a charming neighborhood called Hill Street Terrace. While pedestrians in the traffic tunnels are seldom seen today, this photograph shows several headed toward the Hill Street Tunnel. (Courtesy of CHS.)

This early 1880s photograph shows the residence of Dr. Joseph P. Widney at 321 South Hill Street. Hill Street in the late 19th century had quite a few residences. This one is a two-story Craftsman clapboard house, roomy, but hardly ostentatious. Weeds grow through the sidewalk in front of the house, and the porch is mostly obscured by trees. (Courtesy of CHS.)

Dr. Joseph P. Widney was a physician and public health official and, together with his brother, Robert Maclay Widney, was instrumental in establishing the University of Southern California. He was also the university's second president. Widney was a fervent believer in the superiority of the Anglo-Saxon race, which he espoused in his book, *Race Life of the Aryan Peoples,* published in 1907. (Courtesy of CHS.)

This residence, belonging to Judge Robert Maclay Widney, was on Hill Street between Fourth and Fifth Streets. It is almost completely obscured by the heavy foliage of fan and date palm trees. Robert Maclay Widney, Dr. Joseph Widney's brother, was the city's first real estate salesman. The location of his home was later the site of the Pacific Electric Depot and eventually the Subway Terminal Building, which opened in November 1924 and still stands today. (Courtesy of CHS.)

Judge Robert Maclay Widney, owner of the house pictured above, was a champion of a variety of civic improvements, such as street cars and electric lights. Both Widney brothers played important roles in the development of Los Angeles. (Courtesy of CHS.)

This view of a busy Hill Street looking south from Third Street was photographed in 1903. (Courtesy of CHS.)

A similarly busy view of Hill Street between Third and Fourth Streets was photographed in the early 1930s. (Courtesy of CHS.)

Tim Hawkinson's 1994 Historic Clock Tower (seen here in a 1998 photo) is an imaginary public art work, which can be seen on the parking structure of the Central Market on Hill and Third Streets. The clock dials go in the wrong direction and the roman numerals are reversed. It has no specific references to this location, as a clock tower never existed on this corner. (Courtesy of R. Wallach.)

This 1930s view looks north from Fourth Street at the Luckenbach Building and Hill Street Tunnel. Luckenbach was a noted jewelry company with a long history in the downtown area. By the 1930s, this stretch of Hill Street was completely commercial, with two-story buildings replaced by multi-story ones. (Courtesy of Whittington.)

This transportation themed mosaic on the Subway Terminal Building at 417 Hill Street, photographed in 2000, was done by the Ravenna Mosaic Company. The 1926 building was designed by Schultze and Weaver after a 16th-century Italian prototype. Trains came from Santa Monica and San Fernando; the subway, which brought trains from the west, operated from 1925 to 1955. (Courtesy of R. Wallach.)

This 1998 photo shows the tromp l'oeil mural by Jeff Greene that is painted on the 11th and 12th floors on the Fourth Street side of the Subway Terminal Building. The mural incorporates the building's windows into its design and imitates the arches and pilasters from the Italian Renaissance-styled façade. Two life-size painters on a scaffold appear to be completing the mural. The work, commissioned by owner David Hart in 1986, was the longest public art installation in downtown at that time. (Courtesy of R. Wallach.)

At the turn of the 20th century, Hill Street, particularly south of Fourth Street, became increasingly commercial, as shown in this c. 1905 photo, although it still retained a small town feel. The street remained largely unpaved and accommodated several means of transportation, such as railcars, horse-drawn carriages, and bicycles. The business signs testify to a variety of commercial establishments, such as a café, a haberdashery, an attorney at law, a real estate office, undertakers, etc. (Courtesy of CHS.)

While many large hotels were built along Main Street, the western part of the Historic Core had some of the smaller hotels, such as the Occidental Hotel, seen in this 1910 photo on the east side of Hill between Fourth and Fifth Streets. (Courtesy of CHS.)

Hill Street looking north from the Pacific Electric Depot, between Fourth and Fifth Street c. 1924, bustled with people and traffic. The Occidental Hotel can be seen to the east, looking quite different than it did in 1910. The Los Angeles School of Optometry is seen to the west. (Courtesy of CHS.)

This group photograph shows La Fiesta Tribune Queen, Francisca Alexander, receiving the parade on the Hill Street side of Central Park, (later Pershing Square), c. 1897. La Fiesta de Los Angeles was a carnival first held in April 1894 to celebrate the city's Hispanic heritage. It was also designed to attract tourists on their way to visit San Francisco. The fiesta consisted of parades, a grand ball, and a firework display. It was held annually for 10 years, then a few times during the Great Depression, and revived in 1989 by the merchants association of Broadway as a Cinco de Mayo celebration. (Courtesy of CHS.)

This portrait of the 1897 La Fiesta De Los Angeles Queen, Miss Francisca Alexander, reveals that the queen of La Fiesta was a regal presence, indeed. Miss Alexander appears to be no more than 30 years old. The Alexanders were prominent land developers in Southern California in the 1850s and 1860s. (Courtesy of CHS.)

St. Vincent's College at Sixth and Hill, seen here c. 1880, was a Jesuit college founded in 1865. The first college in Southern California, it was renamed Loyola University in 1911. In 1928 it moved to Westchester, and in 1973 it merged with Marymount College to become Loyola Marymount University. The men in this photograph are all posing, aware that the camera eye is on them. Typical of Los Angeles at the time, the landscape in front of the building has a small fountain surrounded with some sparse vegetation. (Courtesy of CHS.)

This exterior view of Army Headquarters on Sixth Street between Broadway and Hill Streets on the south side was taken in 1889. Imagine this park-like setting in today's Hill Street! (Courtesy of CHS.)

The First Congregational Church on the southwest corner of Hill and Sixth Streets is shown here c. 1900. Founded in 1867, it is the oldest continuously functioning Protestant church in Los Angeles. In 1932 the church moved to Commonwealth Ave. While serving the spiritual needs of its community, the church also participated in real estate transactions, as is indicated by the inscriptions on the back of this photograph: "2 lots bought 1889 for $52,000, sold in 1905 with church building for $76,000. Sold in 5 years for $300,000. T.J. Jones Co." and "The southwest corner of Sixth and Hill streets was sold yesterday by the Congregational Church to a local realty firm for the new high price of $415,000 a rate of $2,766 per front Hill Street foot." (Courtesy of CHS.)

Since the 1970s, the stretch of Hill Street between Sixth and Eighth Streets has functioned as a jewelry center, both wholesale and retail. Some of the buildings, particularly the International Jewelry Center opposite Pershing Square, were built during that time. However, there are many old buildings in the stately Beaux-Arts style, such as this 1920 design by B. Marcus Priteca, photographed in 2004. This building was originally known as the Warner Brothers Downtown Building and Pantages Theater. (Courtesy of R. Wallach.)

This 1931 photo of Hill Street looking south from Seventh Street shows Foreman and Clark men's clothiers in the foreground. The RKO Theater, formerly known as Hill Street Theater, which was part of the Orpheum Circuit, can be glimpsed behind the Garfield Building. (Courtesy of CHS.)

This 1910 photo shows the entrance to the Automobile Club's third office at 753 South Hill Street. The AAA was founded in 1900 as a social club by several auto enthusiasts at a time when cars were an extreme rarity. Its early offices were at various locations on Hill Street. By 1920 the club had 30,000 members, and today it is a national organization serving four million members. (Courtesy of CHS.)

This photo shows Hill and Twelfth Streets looking southwest from the house of Ozro W. Childs in 1875. Childs was a Los Angeles benefactor involved in the establishment of the University of Southern California and the early Los Angeles Opera House. His wife was Queen of La Fiesta de Los Angeles in 1894. Their property was located in what then was countryside. (Courtesy of CHS.)

A fashionably dressed lady stands on the rather non-descript corner of Hill and Twelfth Streets in this 1930s photograph, as if in a *Vogue* advertisement. Norman Klein in *The History of Forgetting* (1997) quotes an elderly interviewee who told him, "We always dressed to go downtown. My parents were Serbian farmers. I think they thought this was Vienna." (Courtesy of Whittington.)

# Five

# PERSHING SQUARE, OLIVE STREET, AND WEST

What is now named Pershing Square is Block 15 on the 1849 survey map drawn by Lieutenant Edward O.C. Ord. At that time, the square was covered with grass and used as a campground by travelers from the pueblo, until the block was dedicated by Mayor Cristobal Aguilar in 1866 as a public square, or plaza, for use by citizens of the city, and named La Plaza Abaja. The Arroyo de Los Reyes that crossed Olive Street near Sixth Street often flooded the surrounding area during rainy seasons. The El Viejo Camino crossed Olive and Fifth Streets, running across the site of the Biltmore Hotel and remained in use almost until the time the square was first planted in 1870. One impetus for creating the public square was that property owners wanted to protect property values on the streets that faced the square: Hill, Fifth, Sixth, and Olive Streets.

The first park plan was designed by a city engineer and later city mayor, Fred Eaton. The square had numerous names, among them Sixth Street Park, St. Vincent's Park, and Central Park. It was called Central Park in 1911 when it was redesigned by John Parkinson, and was renamed Pershing Square in 1918 in honor of America's most distinguished World War I general, John J. Pershing. The park was redesigned in the early 1950s when a three-story garage was built beneath it and reconceived in the early 1990s by architect Ricardo Legorreta and landscape architect Laurie Olin.

The district around Pershing Square, particularly the Seventh Street corridor, developed so dramatically in the 1920s and 1930s that it became a crossroads of the city and attracted the most luxurious hotels and elegant stores. Some of the institutions that moved to Pershing Square during this period remain important to the city, and a number of buildings are listed on the National Register of Historic Places.

As early as 1849, Seventh Street appeared on the Ord survey as part of a southern subdivision of open land. With the completion of the Southern Pacific Railroad to Los Angeles in 1876, churches, residences, and schools were built in this area and around Pershing Square. By the beginning of the 20th century, commercial buildings were constructed in this fast growing downtown sector. Plans to develop Fifth Street as a major east-west corridor for vehicular traffic and public transportation connecting two major downtown Pacific Electric Terminals were interrupted by the Great Depression. The direction of urban development in this part of the Historic Core changed dramatically after that. Twenty-first century revitalization of historic buildings around Pershing Square and the surrounding areas is part of redevelopment of the various districts of downtown Los Angeles.

Visible in this view of the square from Sixth and Hill Streets, c. 1884, are small wood-frame residences, the First Baptist Church, St. Vincent's College, and St. Paul's Episcopal Church. The latter, built in 1883, was the first church in the area. The square was treeless before a beautification campaign was launched in 1870 at a public meeting called to raise subscription funds for what was supposed to be called Los Angeles Park. (Courtesy of CHS.)

This view from the late 1870s is of the *zanja*, an irrigation ditch, which provided water to the square. When the park was created earlier in the decade, a lawn was not planted because water could not be piped so far from downtown Los Angeles. This *zanja* branched from *Zanja Madre* near Requena Street (Market Street), and flowed south before entering the square at Fifth and Hill Streets and exiting at Sixth and Olive Streets. (Courtesy of CHS.)

By 1872 the park had fencing and trees, although the lawn and flowers were not planted until water was piped from downtown. This c. 1888 photograph shows Pershing Square (then called Sixth Street Park) with Olive Street and St. Paul's Episcopal Church in the background. As the new residential section of town, Pershing Square frontage was not considered as elegant as Main Street in the 1880s. (Courtesy of CHS.)

The diagonal walkways in the original park were redesigned when the *zanja* was filled in the mid-1880s and water was piped underground through the business district. The new park design included curved paths, a lawn, and a bandstand, as can be seen in this *c.* 1890 view. (Courtesy of CHS.)

In 1866 the entire north side of Fifth Street was purchased at a municipal auction by Capt. A.M. Hazard and his son-in-law, Harley A. Taft. This house, known as the Mary E. Taft House, was the first building built on the northwest corner of Fifth and Hill Streets, *c.* 1888. Mary E. Taft came to Los Angeles with her father, Captain Hazard, in 1854. (Courtesy of CHS.)

This is a photograph of the second house built by Mary E. Taft on the northwest corner of Fifth and Hill, taken c. 1890. The sign on the porch advertises an osteopathy infirmary. Mary E. Taft sold her homestead to California Club in 1900. Next to her house was Hazard's Pavilion, built in 1887 by Taft's brother and later mayor of the city, Henry T. Hazard. Hazard's Pavilion was the site of prizefights, Chautauqua assemblies, and concerts. This location later became the site of the auditorium. (Courtesy of CHS.)

The intersection of Fifth and Hill Streets is busy with pedestrians, bicycles, horse-drawn carriages, and automobiles in this c. 1905 view of the five-story California Club Building. Utility poles and lines are prevalent in Pershing Square in photographs of this period. Los Angeles was one of the first American cities to have electric streetlights, which were installed in 1882. (Courtesy of CHS.)

This is an exterior view of Hotel Willoughby on the corner of Fifth and Hill Streets, c. 1900. The three-story Victorian hotel was owned by Mrs. E. Hollingsworth and the photo shows a horse-drawn carriage standing in front of the building and electric streetcar tracks on the unpaved street. The first electric streetcars appeared in Los Angeles in 1887. Horse-drawn trolleys stopped running in 1897. (Courtesy of CHS.)

This c. 1913 birds-eye view of Pershing Square shows the completed Los Angeles Philharmonic Auditorium, built in 1906 for the Los Angeles Philharmonic Orchestra. Services of the Temple Baptist Church were also held in the auditorium. It was the home of the orchestra until the Music Center was built in 1964. In fall 2003, the orchestra held its first concert in the new the Walt Disney Concert Hall designed by Frank Gehry. (Courtesy of CHS.)

This undated photograph shows crowds listening to an outdoor concert of opera stars in front of the auditorium building. The caption states that the city was noted for its music. Pershing Square had no lighting before it was redesigned in 1911. After the redesign, broad, diagonal walks replaced winding gravel paths, a fountain replaced the bandstand, and benches dotted the park among the tropical foliage. (Courtesy of CHS.)

This is a panoramic view of Pershing Square from the State Normal School (on the site of today's central library) looking east toward Hill Street, c. 1913. Visible are the auditorium and California Club Building on the left (Fifth Street) and Hotel Willoughby, Boos Bros. Cafeteria, Hotel Portsmouth, and Hotel Lillie across the square on Hill Street. Many properties in the business district, such as the Lillie and Willoughby hotels, were owned by women. (Courtesy of CHS.)

This view of Pershing Square was taken from Hill Street looking west c. 1910. The First Methodist Episcopal Church is in the lower left. Across the square on Olive Street is the Pacific Mutual Life Insurance Building with columns extending above four stories. St. Paul's Episcopal Church and the auditorium building are visible to the right on Fifth Street. (Courtesy of CHS.)

This view shows the exterior of the First Methodist Episcopal Church fronting the square on the northeast corner of Hill and Sixth Streets, c. 1910. The corner entrance has three arched doors with arched stained glass windows directly above. The spire tower and an octagonal tower rise to the right and left. A horse-drawn wagon is parked on the street. (Courtesy of CHS.)

This interior view of the First Methodist Episcopal Church, c. 1905, shows the main floor pulpit, organ, and choir loft. From the ceiling hangs an elegant crystal chandelier. (Courtesy of CHS.)

This c. 1913 view of Olive Street (left) and Pershing Square, taken from Sixth Street looking north, shows snow-covered mountains in the background. The Pacific Mutual Life Insurance Building on the left, with its tall Corinthian columns, is the oldest building standing near Pershing Square today. Also visible are St. Paul's Episcopal Church (left), the auditorium, and the California Club Building on the other side of the park. (Courtesy of CHS.)

109

This photograph shows an exterior view of the Pacific Mutual Life Insurance Building on the corner of Sixth and Olive Streets, c. 1909. The original Beaux-Arts style building of glazed white terracotta had ornamental moldings and a cornice circling the top floor, which was later re-done in the Moderne style. The building was the home office for one of the most important life insurance companies in the west. Between 1908 and 1929 several interconnected buildings were added, and it is now called the Pacific Center. (Courtesy of CHS.)

This panoramic view of Pershing Square, looking south from Hill and Fifth Streets, was taken c. 1925. On the corner of Sixth and Olive Streets are the Heron and Pacific Mutual Life Buildings. The Biltmore Hotel can be seen to the right. The 13-story Heron Building was constructed in 1921 in Renaissance Revival style faced with red and gold bricks, and with columns around the top story windows detailed in terracotta. (Courtesy of CHS.)

The Biltmore Hotel, shown here in a 1930s photograph, opened in 1923 as the largest luxury hotel west of Chicago. Its Beaux-Arts style was popular in American cities at that time and featured red brick and cream colored terracotta. This elegant hotel had meeting rooms off the interior galleria done in different historical styles, with murals and ceiling decorations by Giovanni Smeraldi. The original Olive Street entrance was moved to Grand Street in the mid-1980s. (Courtesy of Whittington.)

This 1930s photograph of Pershing Square looks north toward the Temple Baptist Church Auditorium Building and the new Title Guarantee and Trust Company Building at Fifth and Hill Streets. Built in 1931, the Title Guarantee reflected the relaxation of the original height limits. It had a Gothic tower housing three setbacks for installing floodlights to guide aviators. Designed by John and Donald Parkinson, the building's tower was partly made of a terracotta screen. (Courtesy of Whittington.)

Public art has been in Pershing Square from the beginning of the 20th century. This statue was placed in the square in 1900 in commemoration of the 7th California Infantry during the 1898 Spanish American War. It was removed from the square during the construction of underground parking in the early 1950s along with the statues of the Doughboy (1924) and Beethoven (1932). (Courtesy of CHS.)

The 7th California Infantry monument is shown being moved by a crane into storage while Pershing Square was under construction to build the garage in 1951. The *Examiner* caption states, " 'Guard Duty' Ends." The Heron Building, Pacific Mutual Life, and the Biltmore Hotel are seen in the background along Olive Street. (Courtesy of the *Examiner*.)

The Beethoven monument by Arnold Foerster, dedicated in 1932 to honor the founder of the Los Angeles Philharmonic Orchestra, William Andrews Clark, Jr., was temporarily moved to Griffith Park for the duration of construction of the underground garage at Pershing Square in 1951. The *Examiner* photograph caption of February 8 of that year noted that this is "symbolic of the grim mood of those whose park bench siestas have been interrupted" until the "noisy symphony of progress" ended. (Courtesy of the *Examiner*.)

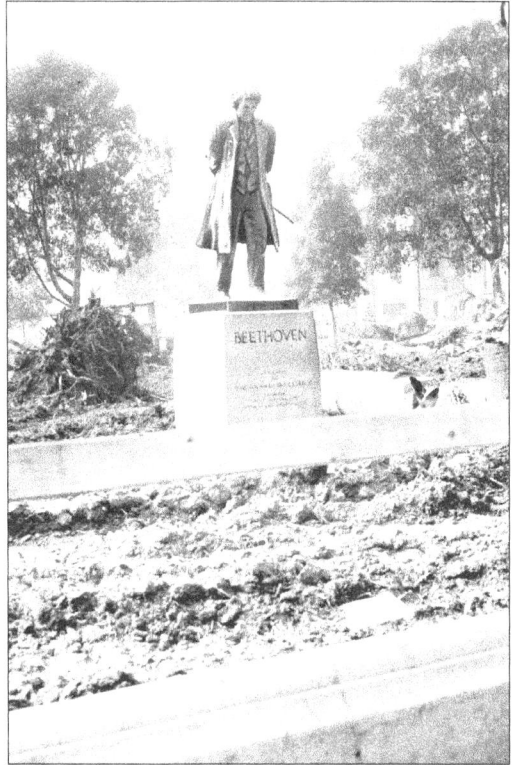

The three bronze sculptures from the early part of the 20th century were repositioned when Pershing Square was redesigned in 1994. Beethoven, the Doughboy, and the 7th California Infantry statues are grouped together at Fifth and Hill Streets near a bench featuring historic postcards. They share the corner with the bronze cannon from the USS *Constitution*, presented to the city in 1935. (Courtesy of L. McCann.)

The caption on this photograph dated April 4, 1951 describes a "pigeon squadron formerly based at Pershing Square," where the birds found handouts at the library. An article published in the *Examiner* on September 14, 1960, noted that a Pershing Square visitor was told by police that he would be sent to jail if he fed the birds. The law prohibiting the feeding of pigeons was designed to prevent them from being a nuisance in downtown. (Courtesy of the *Examiner*.)

The garage construction displaced plants, birds, statues, and citizens who frequented the park. In this 1951 photograph men sit on walls while the square was bulldozed. The 7th California Infantry monument is waiting to be removed. Throughout its history the square was a gathering place for citizens, preachers, and orators. For example, in 1928 there was an investigation of an incident when 37 people were arrested for blocking sidewalks during a demonstration. (Courtesy of the *Examiner*.)

This 1951 photograph shows the newly planted Pershing Square after the construction of the underground three-story garage, billed as the world's largest. In the background is a partial view of the 13-story Park Central Building, which still faces Pershing Square today and the Union Pacific Ticket Office at Sixth and Olive Streets, replaced by the City National Bank. (Courtesy of Whittington.)

Pershing Square, seen in this 2004 photograph looking north from Sixth Street toward Title Guarantee and Trust Company and the parking lot that replaced the auditorium, is a paved plaza designed by Ricardo Legorreta and Laurie Olin. The semicircular bench with an inscription attributed to Cary McWilliams and a tidal fountain are part of a public art work called *Hey Day* by the artist Barbara McCarren. (Courtesy of L. McCann.)

This *c.* 1905 photograph shows the California State Normal School. Los Angeles citizens contributed funds to purchase an orange grove site at this location after the state Assembly approved a teacher's college. The school opened in 1881. In 1914 it moved to Vermont Avenue and in 1927 it became the University of California at Los Angeles, located in Westwood. In 1926 the Los Angeles Central Public Library opened on this site. (Courtesy of CHS.)

This view shows the west entrance of the Los Angeles Central Public Library facing Fifth Street between Grand and Flower, *c.* 1939. The first Los Angeles public library was established in the 19th century and had numerous downtown locations, including city hall, the Homer Laughlin Building, Hamburger's People's Store, and the New Metropolitan Building before the current central library building designed by Bertram Goodhue was built on the site of the State Normal School in 1926. (Courtesy of Whittington.)

The Southern California Edison Building at Fifth and Grand Streets was the office for the utility company. It was completed in 1934 as an art deco steel-framed building with lower stories of granite and upper stories and a central tower faced with terracotta. The interior featured art deco decorative elements, lobby floor and walls faced with different types of marble, and a 1930s mural by Hugo Ballin. Greenhouses, seen on the outside, were added in the 1980s. (Courtesy of L. McCann.)

This *c.* 1927 view shows busy Seventh Street west from Hill Street. Beyond the Warner Building and Pantages Theater is the Bracks Building at 527 West Seventh, built in 1913 in the commercial style with classical and Beaux-Arts detail. The 12-story classical style Union Oil Building at 617 West Seventh (1922) and the 12-story Roosevelt Building at 727 West Seventh, designed in a Beaux-Arts Renaissance style (1925) can also be seen. (Courtesy of CHS.)

This *c.* 1928 view of Seventh and Flower looking west shows the Barker Brothers Building. The Beaux-Arts building, designed by Curlett and Beelman, was the headquarters and retail store for Barker Brothers, then the largest furniture company in Southern California, established in the 1880s in Los Angeles. (Courtesy of CHS.)

This c. 1921 birds-eye view of Seventh Street looking west from Broadway includes the Ville de Paris Department Store seen in the distance. The six-story building was constructed in 1917 on the corner of Olive and Seventh Streets across from Pershing Square in commercial style with classical façade of red brick and white terracotta moldings. Seventh Street was also home to many booksellers. (Courtesy of CHS.)

The Renaissance Revival–style home of the Bank of Italy is pictured here in 1922, around the time of its completion, on the corner of Olive and Seventh Streets. Its three-story façade is punctuated by columns and a distinctive temple front. The streetcar tracks are visible in the street and automobiles are parked on the sides. A number of apartment and commercial buildings surround the bank. (Courtesy of CHS.)

The J.W. Robinson Department Store, built in 1915 at Seventh and Grand Streets, is seen in this c. 1925 photo before it was remodeled in the Moderne style in 1934. The store featured doormen and restrooms with chandeliers. It first opened in 1883 as Boston Dry Goods and relocated to Spring and then to South Broadway before moving to the Seventh Street retail district. (Courtesy of Whittington.)

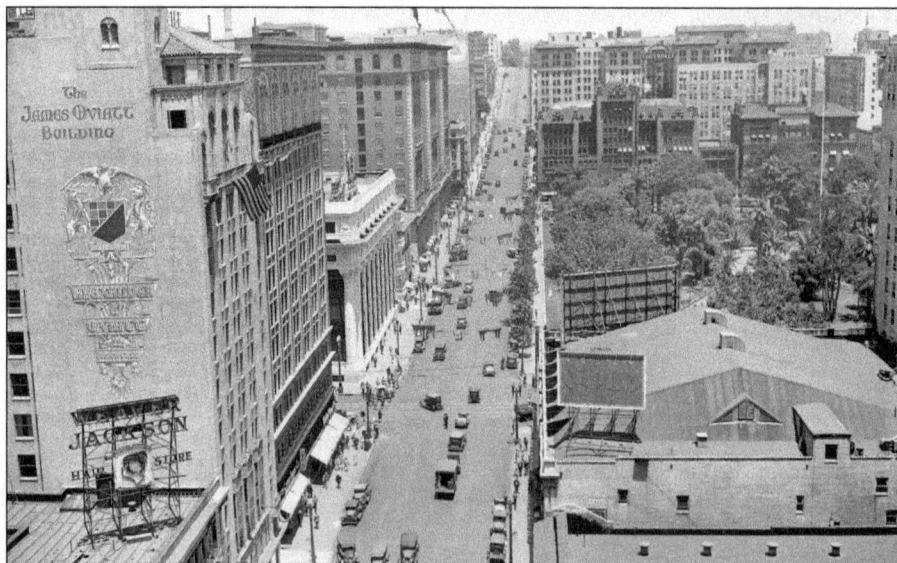

A panoramic view looking north on Olive toward Pershing Square, taken in the 1930s, shows the 13-story James Oviatt Building in the foreground. The building, designed by Walker and Eisen with elements of art deco and Italian Romanesque styles and with glasswork by René Lalique, opened in 1928 as headquarters of the Los Angeles haberdashery Alexander & Oviatt. It included the shop, offices, and a penthouse suite for owner James Oviatt. (Courtesy of CHS.)

The Romanesque Revival 12-story Fine Arts Building by Walker and Eisen at 811 West Seventh Street was built in 1927 with decorative details by Batchelder Studios. The exterior entrance has a two story arch with terracotta decorations and two enormous sculpted figures above the second level windows. The building was restored in the mid-1980s for office space. (Courtesy of the *Examiner*.)

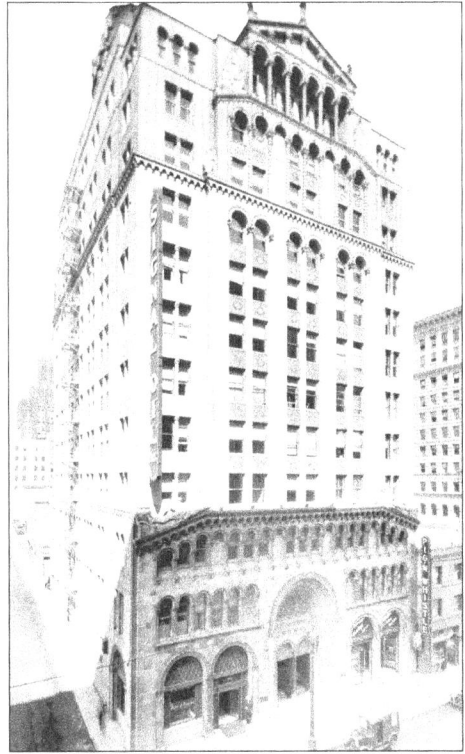

The caption on this 1960 photograph of Clifton's Silver Spoon Restaurant on Olive and Sixth Streets notes that the landmark fell "prey to progress" and became a parking lot. Clifford E. Clinton first opened his Los Angeles chain of cafeterias in 1931. Clifton's Pacific Seas was on Olive Street; another Clifton's was in the 1922 Brock's Jewelers Building at 515 West Seventh Street. Meals were free to those who could not pay. (Courtesy of the *Examiner*.)

Los Angeles Athletic Club, established in 1880 in the Arcadia building on Spring Street, moved to 431 West Seventh Street in 1912 when the Hotel Baltimore was demolished and a new Beaux-Arts style 12-story building was constructed in its stead. It was the first building in Southern California to have an indoor swimming pool. Club membership has included many prominent citizens and admitted women after the Los Angeles Women's Athletic Club closed. (Courtesy of L. McCann.)

Jane Humphreys, who came from a prominent California family and was a longtime Los Angeles businesswoman and philanthropist, chaired a committee which in 1920 organized the Los Angeles Women's Athletic Club. The original design for the building on Flower south of Eighth Street called for "swimming pool, tennis courts, gymnasium, auditorium, library, dining-room, ballroom, baths, massage and hair-dressing parlors, and sleeping quarters." (Los Angeles Times, 1921) It also had an Italian roof garden designed by Florence Yoch. When the club, seen in this c. 1947 photograph, closed, women were admitted to the Los Angeles Athletic Club and took over the tenth floor of that building. (Courtesy of the Examiner.)

The nine-story Embassy Hotel and Auditorium at Ninth and Grand Streets, designed by Thornton Fitzhugh and originally known as the Trinity Auditorium Building, featured a four-story Baroque dome. The Los Angeles Philharmonic Orchestra's premiere performance was conducted at Trinity Auditorium in 1919, around the time of this photograph. Over the years, the auditorium was used for church services, concerts, and conventions, and was purchased in the 1980s by the University of Southern California. (Courtesy of CHS.)

The five-story building on Olympic and Hope was built in 1929 as the Los Angeles branch of the Federal Reserve Bank of San Francisco. It was designed by John and Donald Parkinson in Moderne style and constructed by P.J. Walker Company. This photograph dates from c. 1934. The building is currently undergoing restoration. (Courtesy of Whittington.)

LA REINA DE LOS ANGELES SOBRE EL RÍO DE

This image from 1998 shows the centerpiece of the 1994 triptych by Vitaly Komar and Alexander Melamid. The angel, painted in the style of early Italian Renaissance, also contains elements of Buddhist, African, Native American, and Aztec religions, referencing a variety of cultures that impacted the history of Los Angeles. The triptych is located in the lobby of Library Tower, across Fifth Street from the Central Library. (Courtesy of R. Wallach.)

# BIBLIOGRAPHY

Gates, Worthington, comp. *Los Angeles 1909*. Los Angeles: Western Litho Co., 1909. Courtesy of the Library of Congress American Memory Map Collections: 1500–2004, http://memory.loc.gov/ammem/gmdhtml/gmdhome.html

Gebhard, David and Robert Winter. *Los Angeles: An Architectural Guide*. Salt Lake City, UT: Gibbs-Smith Publisher, 1994.

Guinn, J. M. "The True Story of Central Park." *Annual Publication of the Historical Society of Southern California* 8 (1909–1911): 211–216.

Klein, Norman M. *The History of Forgetting: Los Angeles and the Erasure of Memory*. New York: Verso, 1997.

Longstreth, Richard W. *City Center to Regional Mall: Architecture, the Automobile, and Retailing in Los Angeles, 1920–1950*. Cambridge, Mass.: MIT Press, 1997.

*Los Angeles Times* (1886–Current Files) [newspaper online available from Proquest Historical Newspapers].

Nelson, Howard J. *The Los Angeles Metropolis*. Dubuque, IA: Kendall/Hunt Pub. Co., 1983.

Parkinson, John. *Incidents By The Way: The Boy! What has the Future in Store for Him? What Will Be His Experience?* Los Angeles: Press of Geo. Rice & Sons, 1935.

Soter, Bernadette Dominique. *The Light of Learning: An Illustrated History of the Los Angeles Public Library*. Los Angeles: Library Foundation of Los Angeles, 1993.

Splansky, Joel. *Downtown Los Angeles*. Typescript. 1996.

Robinson, W.W. *The Story of Pershing Square*. Los Angeles: Title Guarantee and Trust Company, 1931.

Pitt, Leonard and Dale Pitt. *Los Angeles A to Z: An Encyclopedia of the City and County*. Berkeley: University of California Press, 1997.

# ABOUT THE
# USC ARCHIVES

The majority of images in this book were made available courtesy of the University of Southern California on behalf of the USC Specialized Libraries and Archival Collections. The authors drew on the following archival collections:

CHS: The California Historical Society/TICOR photographic collection was created by C.C. Pierce, a commercial photographer who documented the growth of Southern California from the late 1800s through the 1930s. The collection concentrates on downtown Los Angeles and includes street, architectural, and panoramic views, but also captures views of seaside cities, rural images, transportation, industrial activity, missions and Southwest Native Americans.

The *Examiner*: The Los Angeles *Examiner* photograph "morgue" is a collection of images, which illustrated articles in the newspaper from the 1930s through the 1950s. The collection includes a wide range of topics and every newsworthy individual from those three decades.

Whittington: The "Dick" Whittington collection was created by a commercial photographer whose studio was one of the eminent photography establishments in Southern California from the mid-1920s through the 1970s. The clientele of the studio included oil, aviation, and automobile companies and large and small business establishments.

AAA: The Automobile Club of Southern California archive contains documents and pictorial materials relating to the club's history since its inception in 1909, and to local and regional architecture, infrastructure, public policy, and cultural and recreational history.

Visit us at
arcadiapublishing.com